Results Matter

Results Matter

Navigating a Lawsuit,
Telling Your Story, and
Achieving a Superior Result

SEAN T. OLSON

EXPERT PRESS

Results Matter: Navigating a Lawsuit, Telling Your Story, and Achieving a Superior Result

Sean T. Olson
Olson Law Firm LLC
2701 Lawrence Street
Suite 118
Denver, CO 80205
303-586-7297
www.olsonlawfirmllc.com

ISBN-13: 978-1-946203-23-6
ISBN-10: 1-946203-23-8

—Disclaimer—

Although the author and publisher have made every effort to ensure that the information in this book was correct at press time, the author and publisher do not assume and hereby disclaim any liability to any party for any loss, damage, or disruption caused by errors or omissions, whether such errors or omissions result from negligence, accident, or any other cause.

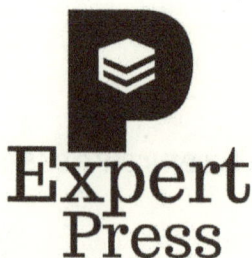

Expert
Press
www.ExpertPress.net

To Lisa, Gray, & Oliver—the reasons for it all

Contents

Introduction

I WROTE THIS BOOK in the hope of showing you what to expect should you decide to pursue a personal injury claim against someone who has harmed you. It's a position in which you didn't ask to be placed. Sadly, it is a decision that will mark the beginning of a long road ahead.

What is a personal injury claim? A personal injury claim is a claim against someone else resulting from being injured in a car accident to being a victim of medical malpractice to slipping and falling on someone else's property through no fault of your own. You are likely reading this book because you have been injured because of someone else's negligence. As a result of something they did—or something they failed to do—you got hurt.

You might feel a little uncomfortable about needing to read something like this, or even about pursuing a personal injury claim. Those feelings are normal, but keep in mind that thousands of people have blazed this path before you. Every single day, people are injured because of something that someone else did. Every single day, there are hundreds of people across the country filing personal injury claims because they were hurt, and the responsible party doesn't want to pay for what they did. They file those claims because it is the only manner in which they can be compensated for their injuries and the harm that has been done to them.

When you're injured as a result of someone else's negligence, you can be harmed in a number of different ways. There will, of course, be pain, suffering, inconvenience and possibly physical disfigurement.

There will be medical bills to pay; there will be time away from work when you are not making money. There will be trips to the doctor's office that need to be paid for. There is the harm that is done to those around you as well. Your spouse, your significant other, your children all suffer when you suffer. Everyone feels the pain, even if it is not the physical pain that you are experiencing.

Money cannot always fully compensate someone for all of those harms, for the lost wages, for the pain, for the disfigurement. But money is the only way that the law can attempt to make you whole. It is the only equalizer we have in our system of justice.

A personal injury case will play out the same way regardless of whether you decide to hire a lawyer to work with you, or whether you try to go it alone. For purposes of this book, let's assume that you have decided to hire a lawyer, the decision that most ultimately make.

A lawyer is going to drive the bus for you. Should you end up taking your case all the way through a jury trial, your case is going to play out, essentially, in three acts. Each new act will begin when the one before it fails to produce a result. Those acts are: 1) the initial investigation; 2) the filing of a lawsuit; and 3) a trial. Inside of each act are many different pieces that fit together to help you and your lawyer build your case so that you can be properly compensated for the harms that have been done to you.

The goal in each act is to tell your story and convince the other side of your righteousness. And if your story fails to convince the person or corporation who did the harm, or it fails to convince their insurance company that you are right, then you're going to need to convince a jury.

A jury trial is truly the only leverage that you have against those very powerful entities aligned against you. The person or company that you want to sue—and the insurance company that represents it—have all been through this process thousands upon thousands of times. They have teams of lawyers lined up against you. Those lawyers are lined up against you to make sure that you are not compensated for the harm that has been done to you. And those lawyers know how the system works. They know how to play the game. They know how to keep money in the pockets of the people who hurt you.

Your ability to put those who harmed you in front of a jury of your peers, of fellow community members, is the only leverage you have. Those entities and those lawyers know that you have that leverage. They know that one day they may be placed in front of those jurors and those jurors could decide in your favor. And they also know that oftentimes, those results—the results after a public trial—are results that they do not want to endure. Your ability to put them there in front of that jury, to take them all the way to the mat, is the leverage you have in convincing them along the way to resolve your case and make up for the harm done.

The role of a personal injury lawyer is to help you through that process. The role of the personal injury lawyer is to help make things right for you, as someone who has suffered a loss, suffered an injury, or suffered some degree of disfigurement. The role of the personal injury lawyer is to be a member of your team, to fight on your side against the very powerful entities who will line up against you.

I became a personal injury lawyer because I believe in that fight. I believe that we have an obligation to look out for one another and to make things right for those who have been harmed through no fault of their own. I believe in standing up for the little guy. That comes from my childhood.

I grew up in a small town in Wisconsin. There I was fortunate to know a community where everyone looked out for one another. If someone was hurt, the members of the community, my neighbors, were the first ones to step forward and bring over hot meals. They were the first ones to make sure the lawn got mowed. They ensured that the work that needed to be done at your place of employment still got done, even in your absence. Everyone looked out for one another, and it helped to create our sense of community.

When I moved to Denver, Colorado, a large city by any definition, I learned that sense of community did not exist everywhere. I found that oftentimes there wasn't a community to look out for each individual, and that injured people, the little guys, could get lost in the shuffle of a big city.

I became a personal injury lawyer to bring back some of that small community, to ensure that each individual has someone to look out for them, even when no one else will. I wanted my neighbors to know that they have someone who is willing to stand by their side and fight with them to make sure that when they are hurt as a result of someone else's negligence, there is someone there who will make it right. That's why I do what I do. I hope this book provides some insight as to the things that we have to do in order to get there.

I didn't set out in life with the goal of becoming a lawyer. I received my undergraduate degree in journalism and mass communication. After graduating, I went on to work as a photojournalist and writer in the television news business and documentary industries. I spent the first decade of my working days behind a camera, traveling the country, traveling the world, meeting people, and telling their stories. But in that role as a photographer, I was always a bystander. It seemed my ability to truly help those people was limited.

I wanted to be more than a bystander to the things going on around me. Law school, and being a lawyer, was the way I wanted to make that change. And being a trial lawyer, I found, was one way that I could continue telling others' stories. In doing so, I could actually make change and do good on behalf of those that I would represent.

Being a personal injury lawyer—being a trial lawyer—gives me the opportunity to tell stories in the same way that I did when I worked behind the camera. It gives me the opportunity to get to know my clients, to learn their story, to help them tell their story even better than they did before, and to take that story and present it to a jury of their community members. I get to help those jurors understand who my client is, what happened to them, why it affected them so much, and why they, as jurors, should do something about it.

That is why I became a personal injury attorney and it is why I continue to tell the stories of injured Americans today.

It's All About the Story

Stories are important. They are the most efficient means by which to impart knowledge. And when told well, stories are the most efficient means by which to move people to action.

A human's short term memory is capable of holding on to seven to nine facts for about thirty seconds. Those facts are stored in a single part of the brain. After thirty seconds, if nothing is done with those facts, the brain discards them and prepares itself for the introduction of a new set of seven to nine facts on which to hold for another thirty seconds. It can be an endless routine.

But when facts are shared inside of a story, multiple parts of the human brain become activated. Those seven to nine facts, instead of being stored in a single location, get stored in multiple locations. The brain creates associations between each of those locations. And in doing so, the brain creates memories. It's why decades after hearing Little Red Riding Hood, you can probably recall with little difficulty the names of each of the characters, but at the same time have trouble remembering what you had for lunch yesterday.

A well-told story, however, does more than just enable someone to remember facts. A well-told story can move a person to action. While listening to a story, the human brain actually undergoes physical changes through the release of hormones. A story that creates suspense causes the release of dopamine, responsible for that powerful feeling you get after watching a good action film. Dopamine increases focus, increases motivation, and further increases memory capabilities.

Oxytocin is released in the brain when a story causes you to feel empathy. Oxytocin is the same chemical the brain releases when you fall in love. Oxytocin increases trust, increases bonding, and increases levels of generosity.

The brain releases endorphins when a story makes you laugh. Endorphins feel good. Endorphins also make you more creative, more relaxed, and more focused.

Your story, told well, will release all of those hormones— and maybe more—in the brains of those who hear it. So when someone hears your story—the story of who you are, how you were injured, and how your injuries affected you—they are moved to make it right.

That makes your story the vehicle that will move your case from beginning to end. It is my hope that your story ultimately moves an insurance adjustor, another lawyer, or a group of jurors to make things right. And in the pages that follow, I hope to provide you with a better understanding of how that will happen.

ACT ONE:

PRE-LITIGATION

Chapter One

Finding an Attorney

WHEREVER YOU LIVE, there are likely thousands of attorneys for you to choose from to represent you in your personal injury case. You cannot walk out the door these days without seeing a billboard, hearing a radio ad, or seeing a television advertisement for a personal injury attorney who claims they will fight for you. Their ads are everywhere.

You need to find the attorney who is right for you and right for your case. And that can be a very difficult job. But it is also the single most important job that you will undertake in your journey on your personal injury case.

Can I afford an attorney?

This is often the first question asked, and the fear of not being able to afford representation prevents many people from seeking an attorney when they need one. The short answer is yes, you <u>can</u> afford an attorney. It is important to know that most personal injury attorneys will take your case on what is called a <u>contingency fee basis</u>. That means that the attorney will get paid out of your settlement or your verdict.

You do not have to pay out-of-pocket to hire a lawyer on a contingency fee basis. Were that the case, and clients had to pay by the hour, very few people could afford attorneys. So the contingency fee becomes the great equalizer—giving you the ability to hire an attorney who has as much education and as many skills as the attorneys that the insurance companies are going to hire to work against you. And your attorney can start working for you immediately, regardless of how much money you have in the bank.

When you hire an attorney on a contingency fee, the attorney will not get paid until you get paid. At the end of the day, should you find a settlement, or receive a jury verdict, the contingency fee allows your attorney to be paid a percentage of the amount that is collected for you. In other words, the more your attorney gets for you, the more your attorney gets paid. The inverse, of course, is also true—if you receive nothing, your attorney gets nothing as well. In other words, your lawyer takes on the risks of your case with you.

The same can usually be said for costs in the case—out-of-pocket expenses that someone has to pay for. Those costs often include court filing fees, deposition costs, investigators, and expert fees. All those things can add up. Many times, and in most states, personal injury attorneys can front those costs for you. That means the attorney will pay for them out of his or her own pocket and make sure those costs are covered—again allowing you to have the same level of representation that the insurance companies have, regardless of whether you have the ability to pay for it or not.

The point is, <u>don't let the fear of expense keep you from consulting an attorney or hiring one if you need one</u>. The system is set up so that your attorney can represent you without emptying your wallet at the same time.

When should I hire an attorney?

It is important to talk to a lawyer as soon as you know that you have been harmed. That is because you are always going to have to comply with a <u>statute of limitations</u>, which is the amount of time that the law allows you to bring a lawsuit against a person or corporation who has injured you. As a society, we have decided that we do not want the liability for an accident to hang with a person for the remainder of their days on this earth. No one wants to be greeted on their ninetieth birthday with the news that they are finally being sued for an auto accident that occurred when Carter was president. As a result, legislatures in every state have determined there are specific time limits under which you can bring a lawsuit.

Usually the statute of limitations is a matter of a year or two, sometimes more. If you wait too long to bring a lawsuit, and you wait beyond the statute of limitations in your state, you will forever lose your ability to bring a lawsuit.

I once had a client come speak with me about an injury that he had suffered at the hands of a doctor who undoubtedly had done things improperly. The doctor's improper actions had taken away this client's ability to walk for the rest of his life. Unfortunately, the client waited six years after the injury occurred to find a lawyer. He asked me, "Do I have a case?"

It was one of the saddest conversations I have ever had. My answer had to be, "You undoubtedly have a case, but you needed to bring your case four years ago in order to be compensated for your injuries." Unfortunately, that client had gotten advice from someone close to him—someone he knew well and trusted—that he could wait and he could hold out a little while longer before he made an effort to contact an attorney. That advice was simply wrong. As I watched tears streaming down my client's cheeks, I had to tell him that there was nothing I could do for him.

Do not make his mistake. Speak with an attorney early on. Find out early whether or not you have a case. A delay could literally be the difference between finding justice for your injuries or finding no justice at all.

There is another important reason to consult an attorney early on. In the aftermath of an accident or any sort of incident in which you have been harmed, there is always the possibility of evidence being lost over the course of time. That can happen because someone intentionally destroys the evidence, knowing they have done wrong, or it can simply happen because evidence is lost in the normal course of events. Evidence like security camera video, for example, may simply be overwritten after a period of 30 days or 45 days. The evidence could be lost when someone just does not put the file where it should go, because they do not know that it's important. Talking to an attorney can often stop things like that from happening.

Attorneys have the ability to prevent the destruction of evidence. If you bring an attorney in early enough, your ability to preserve evidence is strengthened. The last thing in the world you want is to delay speaking to an attorney only to find out that all the evidence you thought would help your case no longer exists, simply because you waited for too long.

Evidence can also be lost through no fault of anyone. An accident scene changes over the course of time. Days pass, months pass, the weather changes, snow falls, water flows over an accident scene, and it changes. Even the ability to take pictures, photographs, and videos can be impaired with the course of time. Witnesses' memories are impaired with the course of time. No one remembers things as well two years down the road as they did the day after they witnessed something. Any time you can reach out to witnesses, any time you can take photographs of the way something exists at the time, and any time you can see a scene close in time to an event, the better your story will be told, and the stronger your case will be. So do not delay in consulting with an attorney, even if you do not know yet whether you want to hire one or not.

Who's the right attorney for me?

For many people, being injured in an accident and having to speak with an attorney is the first occasion they have ever have to encounter an attorney. It can be intimidating. But it is important to remember that attorneys are people, too.

I recently met with a new client and her boyfriend. When her boyfriend walked in and shook my hand and said hello, he immediately mentioned that I was not at all what he expected. When I asked him why, he said, with a very surprised look on his face, "Well, you're just a person; you're actually someone I can talk to. I had no idea it was going to be this way." He was right. I was just a person.

So don't forget that attorneys are all human. They all get up and put on their pants the same way you do every single day. Keep that in mind when you meet with them. Don't be intimidated by their title. Ask them questions. Get to know them a little bit. Share some stories. Make sure that they are the right fit for you.

The next question you have to ask yourself, then, is who is the best attorney for me?

First, it is very important to find someone who knows about cases like yours. The lawyer who handled your divorce or drafted your will might not know the first thing about what goes into a personal injury case. Not all lawyers have the same experience. Not all lawyers have the same education. Not all lawyers have the same set of skills.

Finding a lawyer who knows, first of all, what a personal injury case is and what goes into it, is very important. It is also important that the attorney has experience in the kind of case that you are bringing to them. A car accident case is not the same as a medical malpractice case. An airplane incident is not the same as a slip and fall. And oftentimes, the only way lawyers have to learn how a particular case will work, is to have experience working those kinds of cases.

Look around; ask friends and acquaintances who have been through personal injury claims for their recommendations. A friend's experience may be representative of the kind of service you will receive from the same attorney. And if that friend was happy with the service they received, that may be a good sign.

When you finally meet with an attorney or two, there are several important questions that you should ask.

Who will be your point of contact with the law firm? This is the first question you should ask of any attorney. Law firms come in many different shapes and sizes, from sole practitioners (attorneys who practice law on their own) to large firms with dozens of attorneys and hundreds of staff. When you meet with an attorney or anybody from those law firms, you need to know who you are going to be speaking to. Will you get to talk to a lawyer, or will you be talking to a paralegal or a legal assistant? Is there someone at the firm who simply specializes in talking to clients while someone else behind the scenes does all the work?

It is important for you to know that because some people have different levels of comfort with the manner in which their case will be handled. Some people don't care if their case is handled by a firm with dozens of attorneys and hundreds of staff members. They will not care if they do not see a lawyer until they get to trial. For some people, that is okay. Others are not going to be comfortable with that arrangement. Some people want more direct contact with their lawyer. They might require the ability to sit down and tell their lawyer their story, so that their lawyer understands exactly what it is that they have gone through. They want their *lawyer*, not an assistant, to understand exactly how an accident affected them and exactly how that accident has affected those around them. Those lawyers are more likely to be found in small firms and medium-sized firms. So your job is to determine what sort of lawyer and what sort of firm you are comfortable with, and seek that person out.

How comfortable are you with your contact person? Once you have determined what kind of firm you prefer, and have sought those firms and lawyers out, there are more questions to ask of the lawyers that you are speaking with. You have to ask yourself honestly how comfortable you are with this person that you will be talking to. You must keep in mind that you will be disclosing a great deal of personal information—information that you might not want to share with anybody else. You are going to be inviting that attorney, that paralegal, or that legal assistant into some of the darkest corners of your life, where your real pain resides. And being comfortable enough with that person to be honest with them is going to be of the utmost importance.

Remember this: A personal injury case is a marathon, not a sprint. It will take a good amount of time, even if you settle your case, for your case to be resolved. Some cases might get settled in a matter of a few months. Other cases might literally take a decade to be resolved in front of a jury. You have to be prepared for the long race. And you have to know that the attorney that you hire is going to be with you that entire time. If you are not comfortable with that person on your team, the distance of that race will seem much greater. It could ultimately impact the resolution of your case.

Does your attorney know their way around a courtroom? Once you have found someone you are comfortable with, you have to ask about that attorney's courtroom experience. Do they try cases? Have they tried cases? There are many lawyers out there who claim to be trial lawyers who have never actually set foot in a courtroom. It is your job to ask those lawyers about their level of trial experience.

Why does that matter? Insurance companies know which attorneys are willing to go to trial and they know who is not. If an insurance company knows you have a lawyer who does not want to take your case to trial, the insurance company will use that information against you in the long run. Remember that standing in front of a jury and telling your story is the only leverage you have over those insurance companies and over those corporations who have done you harm. And if the insurance company and the corporations know that you are not willing to use that leverage, you will not be fully compensated. So anytime you hire a personal injury attorney, it is important to know that you are hiring one who knows how to try a case and one who is willing to do so on your behalf.

Sometimes you may find a lawyer that you really like—one you are comfortable with, who you know will be your point of contact, and who has been in a courtroom many, many times—but that lawyer might not have experience in the kind of case you have. In those sorts of circumstances, it is always possible for your lawyer to hire a second lawyer. We call it associating with counsel or co-counseling. What that means is your attorney has found another attorney that your attorney is comfortable with, who knows how your kind of case works. The two of them can work as a team to ensure that your case is worked up properly.

It is important to note that in those circumstances, the amount of money you pay to your attorneys does not change. The fee that you agree upon with your attorney initially is the same fee you are going to pay, whether you have one attorney or 50 attorneys working on your case. And associating with more attorneys might be another way to bring strength to your case.

Once you have gone through those questions, once you have had conversations with the attorney of your choosing, and you have decided this is the right person to tell your story, then it is time to move on to your second step: providing your attorney with as much information as you can to get things started.

Chapter Two

Information Gathering

SO YOU HAVE SELECTED an attorney and you have scheduled your first meeting. That initial meeting with your attorney may take place at the lawyer's office, but it could also take place at your home, at a coffee shop, or some other place where you are comfortable.

In that meeting, it is important to bring all the information you might have, whether that is photographs, names of witnesses, or documents regarding your lost wages. One of the things that can be most helpful for an attorney is your medical records. If you can take the time to collect those even before going to see an attorney, it will help your attorney evaluate both your damages and potential liability for those who caused you harm. Before walking into that lawyer's office, collect as much information as you can. Make that conversation as fruitful as you possibly can by bringing information to the table.

Your first question will probably be: Do I have a case? That is typically the first question that everyone has when they have been injured or suffered some kind of loss. It's usually the first question I hear when I see a new client, and it is understandable. Of course you want to know right away whether you have a viable case, but your attorney may not be able to answer that question immediately.

There are three things your attorney will want to know to help determine whether you have a case. They are:

1. Have you actually been damaged or injured?

2. What is the value of the damages that you've suffered?

3. Are the damages collectible?

Let's look at each of these in more detail.

Have you been damaged or injured?

In terms of the first question, it is important for you to know that inconvenience is usually not enough. It simply doesn't make economic sense to spend thousands of dollars on a personal injury case if all you are going to get back for the inconvenience that you have been put through is $100.

In order to determine if you have been damaged or injured enough to make it worthwhile to bring a case, there are several places for your lawyer to look. The first is medical bills—what kinds of medical costs have you already incurred, and what other medical bills do you anticipate?

Another is any out-of-pocket costs you may have incurred, like medications, medical devices, or other items you would not have otherwise had to pay for. You may have missed work, missed wages, and missed opportunities—all of which may be compensable.

Your lawyer can also consider intangibles like pain and suffering. He or she can consider any kind of physical disfigurement that you may have suffered as a result of an accident. That could be anything from scarring to the loss of a limb or any other way that you are physically different now than you were before the accident.

Your lawyer may also consider the intangibles of a spouse who's been affected by your injuries. The attorney will take into account whether that spouse has lost out on what we call in the legal world "consortium," which is essentially the intimate partnership that you and your spouse share. If your injuries have resulted in a loss of intimacy between you and your partner, that may be considered a recoverable harm as well.

What is the value of your damages?

After establishing what those damages are, your attorney is going to try to make some determination of the value of those damages. Your attorney has to do that in order to know whether it is worth your time, and whether it is worth your attorney's time, to try to collect on those damages. Not every case is the same. If you can only show that you've been damaged by $1,000, it might not make economic sense for you to pursue a personal injury claim because you are almost guaranteed to spend more than $1,000 of your time on fighting the case. You are almost guaranteed to spend more than $1,000 paying for the things necessary to fight your case. You are almost guaranteed to incur more than $1,000 in frustration along the way. It is important to look at whether the economics of your case make sense. If they do—if there's money to be made and it makes sense to compensate you for the harms that have been done to you—then you and your attorney might make the decision to move forward to the last question, which is whether those damages are collectible.

Are your damages collectible?

In order to determine whether those damages are collectible, your lawyer first has to ask if there is, in fact, someone to sue. Did someone else cause your injuries in the first place? Or were your injuries caused because of some negligence on your own part? Did you turn left in front of that semi-truck when you shouldn't have? Were you not looking where you were walking when you tripped over the broken side walk?

In other words, was it your fault, or was it someone else's? If it is someone else's fault, is it more than one person or more than one corporation's fault? Were there multiple players involved, each taking an action which led to your injuries?

If someone did undertake some action that led to your injuries, were those actions, what we call under the law, negligent? In deciding whether someone has acted negligently, the law asks whether that person did a thing that a reasonable person would not do or failed to do something that a reasonable person would do. In other words, was the person careful or not?

It is rare that you will be able to provide in a first meeting with an attorney all the answers that your attorney needs to answer the question of who was at fault. But that meeting will, at a minimum, give you an idea of the homework you need to do in order to answer the questions that your attorney needs answered. It is your attorney's job during those meetings to determine whether your case is as you think it is, or if there is more to it.

It is important for an attorney to look beyond the obvious borders of your case to determine who is responsible, where they are responsible, and how much they might be responsible for. It often happens in an initial meeting that we determine there is more to someone's case than that person might think. It becomes the attorney's job then to continue asking questions to answer the issues that are presented. It becomes the attorney's job to do additional homework to find out who it is that might be responsible for your injuries, and how much responsibility those people might have.

For example, in one case that I worked on, the client was badly injured as the result of a drunk driving accident. The attorney who got the case initially realized there was very little insurance money to be had from the driver who had caused the client's horrific injuries. But by looking further into the case and by asking more questions, the attorney realized that there were in fact others who were responsible for the client's injuries. The responsible parties included the bars who had served the driver alcohol well after that driver was intoxicated, and even the hotel that kicked the client and the driver out at three o'clock in the morning with no alternative form of transportation to be had. As a result of looking beyond the obvious borders of the case, the attorney was able to find other responsible parties, and ultimately get full compensation for his client's injuries even though there was very little insurance money to initially cover things.

If you can determine that there was, in fact, a negligent person or entity that caused your harm, you can then move on to the last question in the equation, which is: Can that person make it right? In other words, is there an insurance policy that the other driver owns? Is there an insurance policy that the corporation has to cover the acts of its employees? If there is no insurance policy, are there assets that the other person might have? Sometimes, sadly, the answer to that question is no. The other driver doesn't have an insurance policy and doesn't have any assets of their own. The corporation, in fact, is bleeding money on a weekly basis and is about to file for bankruptcy the next day. Under those circumstances, it may do you no good to pursue a personal injury action, because there may not be a chance that you can ever recover anything for your injuries at the end of the day.

If, on the other hand, you can answer that question in the affirmative, that the damages you have suffered are in fact collectible against the negligent party (or possibly against an insurance policy that you own), then your attorney can move on to figuring out how to make things right for you.

The lesson here is even if you have some question in your mind about whether you have a case, talk to an attorney so that you can look to the corners and look outside of what is obvious, to determine whether or not you can actually be compensated for the harm that has been done to you. Do not assume you have all the answers. An attorney who has been through it before may have more.

Wrongful death cases

We should point out that wrongful death cases are also personal injury cases, though they are somewhat different from regular negligence claims. Wrongful death claims can be brought if an individual actually dies as a result of someone else's negligence or fault, as opposed to being simply injured. Wrongful death claims can be brought by certain members of the deceased person's family including a spouse, children, and others who may have relied upon the deceased person while that person was alive.

While the laws vary from state to state, generally speaking, wrongful death statutes allow for the recovery of economic damages resulting from the death of a deceased individual. That means the loss of income or other economic support that would have been received by the survivor had the deceased individual not been killed. But wrongful death statutes also sometimes limit the damages a jury can impose against the negligent person or corporation, often setting a low cap on non-economic damages. Ironically, it is often less expensive for the at-fault party in an accident to kill someone than to injure someone. It is always important to note that wrongful death actions often have a different statute of limitations from other negligence actions. So if you have a wrongful death claim it is important to talk to your lawyer about the appropriate time to file a lawsuit.

Other ways your attorney can help

It is a sad reality in our society that sometimes people don't have access to the medical care that they need to help them through their injuries. Maybe you do not have insurance that would enable you to get the medical care you need. Maybe your insurance doesn't permit you to get medical care in the time that you need it. Your attorney may be able to assist you with those issues as well by pointing you in the direction of medical care providers who will provide medical care to you while your case is pending.

We often call that providing medical care on a lien. What that means for you is that your doctor—your new doctor —might treat you without asking for any payment up front, but knowing that at the end of the day when your personal injury case is resolved that the doctor will get paid from the proceeds of your personal injury case, similar to the way your attorney will.

After the meeting

Once you've had that first meeting with your attorney, you've answered the questions you can, and you've provided your attorney with as much information as you can, your attorney will then be able to go to work on the next phase of the case—investigating and answering as many of the questions about your case as she possibly can, and getting ready to file a lawsuit and maybe even take your case to a trial.

A Case in Point: Joe's Story

Let's take the opportunity to follow a case through this process:

Joe Miller was driving home from a night out with his wife, Mary, when they were hit by a tractor trailer that ran a red light. The truck hit the passenger side of their car and, in the crash, Mary was killed instantly. Joe was seriously injured and was unconscious when first responders arrived. Paramedics took Joe by ambulance to the nearest emergency room, where doctors diagnosed Joe with a concussion and broken bones in both legs.

By looking at Joe's personal effects, the police were able to contact Joe's brother David, whom Joe had listed as his emergency contact. David rushed to the hospital to look after his brother. David realized right away that Joe would need a lawyer to help him through the aftermath of this tragic accident. So David contacted an old classmate, Jonathan Stone, a personal injury lawyer.

After doctors released Joe from the hospital, and following Mary's funeral, Joe had his first meeting with Jonathan. He brought his medical records and the police report from the accident. Joe told Jonathan that he was going to need ongoing treatment for the injuries to his legs. He had undergone surgery on both legs, and a rod had been inserted in his left leg. Joe's doctors had told Joe he would likely have a permanent limp and some degree of pain in both legs for the rest of his life.

Right after his meeting with Joe, Attorney Stone called in his investigator, Dale Wilson, who immediately started gathering information about Joe and Mary's accident.

Chapter Three

Investigation

THE INITIAL MEETING provides an attorney with an idea of what your case looks like. It also provides us with a very good idea of what is missing. In other words, we learn what questions need to be asked. We learn what materials need to be collected and what witnesses need to be interviewed. Once we know what is missing and what questions need to be answered, the next step in your case is to conduct an investigation, and to the best of our ability get answers. There are several common steps in the investigation process.

Collecting documents

One of the first tasks will be the collection of documents. Those documents can take many different forms. They can include public documents like police reports or investigative reports by a governmental agency of some variety.

Obtaining those records is often more difficult than it would necessarily appear at first blush. Public documents often require submitting open records requests or filling out forms at the particular entity that possesses the records. If a governmental agency doesn't want to hand over records, getting them can require its own court case. Your attorney may have to file an action in a court in order to compel the governmental agency to turn those documents over to you. So that process itself can sometimes take weeks or months.

If you have a personal injury case, more than likely you have medical records floating around out in the world. They will be sitting on doctors' desks. They will be sitting on doctors' hard drives. They will be sitting on hospitals' hard drives. All those medical records also need to be collected.

Most of the time, getting medical records is simply a matter of filling out a request and sending that particular request off to the hospital, doctor's office, or other entity that possesses the records. As you can imagine, hospitals and doctor's offices get requests for medical records all the time. As a result, it can sometimes take a long time for the hospital or doctor's office to simply process your request, get the records together, and send them out. So, securing medical records can sometimes be as challenging as getting public documents, even though federal law provides you a right to your own records.

Sometimes we find that medical records do not exist where we thought they existed. Perhaps you received medical care at an office that you did not remember, maybe immediately after the accident or incident. Maybe you were seriously injured and were taken to an emergency room that you do not recall. Oftentimes, we will discover that information during the course of trying to collect your records, and that can extend the process even more. Ultimately, however, record collection should not take more than a couple of months. In the grand scheme of things, that may seem like a long time. In terms of a lawsuit, it is a very short period of time.

Investigating the incident

Your attorney may also want to <u>hire an investigator</u> to look into your accident. The role of that investigator is to talk to people, find evidence, examine the scene, and gather information on your attorney's behalf. It is important to sometimes use an investigator because an investigator is independent of your attorney. Your attorney cannot be a witness for you down the road in a courtroom trial, but an investigator can testify about things that investigator learns. As a result, attorneys often hire investigators to go out into the world and ask the kinds of questions that the attorney themselves would want to have asked. Once the investigator gets those answers and collects that information, that investigator can later serve as your witness should you ever have to go to a hearing or a trial where the investigator's findings become important.

Importantly, investigators can cost money. While your attorney may want to use one, and you may want to use one, investigators can sometimes be cost prohibitive. Any time an attorney is weighing the options as to how to collect that information, and the option of an investigator is present, the attorney has to look at the value of your case, in order to determine how much money it might be worth to spend investigating the facts of your matter.

Not every case is worth having an investigator. For example, if your damages are $10,000, it would not make sense to spend $11,000 to hire an investigator to collect every tiny piece of evidence that may exist. However, if your damages are $500,000, it may very well make sense to hire an investigator for $11,000 to collect as much information as possible to make your case as strong as possible.

Talk to your attorney about hiring an investigator. Your attorney's been there before. Your attorney knows investigators and knows what kind of work they can do, and how much that work will cost. Have a discussion with your attorney about whether it would be worthwhile bringing an investigator on as part of your team.

Asking the experts

Your attorney may also have to hire <u>expert witnesses</u> at the outset of your case. Expert witnesses are typically doctors, scientists, or engineers—people with specialized knowledge in a particular field.

In a personal injury case, one expert often relied on is an <u>accident reconstructionist</u>—typically an engineer of some variety. Accident reconstructionists reconstruct an accident in order for the parties involved to determine what happened, how it happened, who made it happen, and what could have prevented it from happening. Often, accident reconstructionists will revisit a scene where an accident occurred. They will take measurements, they will take photos, and they will learn what the layout of the land is. Then a reconstructionist will take the information they collect from the scene and compare it to the information that may be in investigative reports, witness reports, and your own accounting of what occurred. The reconstructionist will use all of that information to make determinations based upon those facts, and, at the end of the day, should have the ability to tell the story of what happened.

In the context of an auto accident, one of the most common scenarios under which an accident reconstructionist would be used, the accident reconstructionist will try to duplicate the speed at which the vehicles were traveling, the direction from which the vehicles were traveling, and the particular spot at an accident location where the accident occurred. When the reconstructionist has made those determinations, he or she can give you an idea of exactly what went wrong to cause the accident itself.

When you are armed with that sort of information, you know exactly what the strengths of your case are, and potentially the weaknesses. Sometimes the accident reconstructionist may determine that in fact you were at fault, and you do not have a case, and that's okay. It is important to learn your level of fault early in a case rather than later when a significant investment of time and money has already been made.

But an accident reconstructionist may also determine that it was someone else who was at fault and the reconstructionist may determine that person was in the wrong. When that happens, your attorney will know who the proper parties are on the other side from whom to try to collect damages.

In a medical malpractice case, your attorney will often hire a <u>medical malpractice consultant</u>, typically another doctor who practices in the same field as the doctor you believe caused harm through his or her negligence. It is often difficult to find a doctor in the same community as the doctor who caused you harm to serve as a consultant and form an opinion about the care another doctor provided. Doctors are a small community, and if they start pointing the finger at one another they tend to lose friends quickly, so they try not to do that. If your case needs a medical malpractice consultant, your attorney will often look outside of your community—and possibly even outside of your state—to find someone who is willing to look at your case, objectively point out what went wrong and why it went wrong, and provide an opinion on whether or not it was negligence.

Your attorney may use a variety of methods to find these medical malpractice consultants. Sometimes the attorney may simply know a doctor out of state who has experience in matters similar to yours, and can call them up and ask them to review your case and form an opinion as to what happened and why it happened. And sometimes your lawyer will rely on other lawyers to help them find a doctor with the sort of expertise that you need. Like most other expert witnesses, medical malpractice consultants are expensive, and you will want to talk to your attorney again about whether it makes sense to consult with one in your case.

Product liability experts, like accident reconstructionists, are typically engineers in a particular field. Product liability experts can look at a particular product that you believe caused you harm and determine if the product was defective, if the product was dangerous the way it was made, or if it was the user's fault that caused the harm. Product liability experts can take a product apart and determine how it works, why it works, and what potentially went wrong along the way to make it hurt you.

Product liability experts come in a variety of different forms, depending on their education, their background, and their experience. As a result, product liability experts may take longer to find, so it is always important if you believe you have been harmed by a product defect to give your lawyer plenty of time to find someone who can look at your case and tell you how strong your case might be.

Talking to experts who have knowledge about your case—about what happened and how it happened, and what sorts of damages occurred as a result of what happened—can be a very valuable tool in going forward with your case.

Like investigators, however, experts are expensive. Experts' bills can pile up much faster than an investigator's bills. As you can imagine, doctors bill a lot for their time. Physicists from Harvard with 33 degrees do not come cheap. As a result, you and your attorney will have to have discussions about whether it makes sense to hire an expert witness, and make an investment in that expert's time. In other words, again, if your case is only worth a few thousand dollars, it wouldn't make sense to hire a doctor for $10,000 at the outset to opine as to whether malpractice had occurred in your particular surgery. It wouldn't make sense to spend $20,000 on an expert accident reconstruction if your case is only worth $5,000. But the higher your damages are, the more likely it is that hiring an expert early on will be valuable. An expert who can form opinions and tell you exactly what happened, how it happened, and what ultimately occurred, could be key to your case strategy. It may make the difference between years of litigation or an early resolution of your case. So it is important to speak with your attorney about whether the investment in an expert's time is worth it in your case.

Even if your damages are low, and you and your attorney determine that it is not worth hiring an expert at this stage, that does not necessarily mean you have a weak case or a case that shouldn't be pursued. It all comes down to making good business decisions at this stage in the game. No attorney wants to see their client lose money in the course of a lawsuit. Your attorney always wants you to walk away with money that helps to compensate you for the wrong that has been done to you. If your attorney tells you that it is not worth hiring an expert, do not take it personally. Your attorney is simply trying to make good decisions on your behalf.

Consulting other lawyers

Your attorney may also want to talk to other lawyers. Other lawyers often have expertise that your lawyer may not necessarily have. They may have experience in a particular case that your lawyer does not. Relationships with other attorneys who have different skills and different experiences are what sometimes what make going to a lawyer a valuable act on your behalf. For example, I recently had a medical malpractice case where my client's gallbladder surgery went horribly wrong. It just so happened I had a friend from law school who also practiced in the field of medical malpractice, who had done a very similar case a short time ago. I was able to consult with him. In fact, we felt so strongly about his experience that we brought him in, and he ended up serving as co-counsel in the case. Having him at our side, someone with experience doing the exact same thing that we were doing at that moment in time, proved to be invaluable to us when we ultimately went to trial and had to try the case to a jury.

Talking to other lawyers also becomes important in product liability cases when suing a defendant who has been involved in cases before. Oftentimes, attorneys who have been involved in a previous case will know where that defendant keeps documents. They will know what players from the defendant's corporation or company may have knowledge about the particular case, and they may know about what sort of knowledge the defendant has about the case.

So talk to your lawyer about talking to other lawyers. It does not necessarily mean your lawyer is inexperienced or not as good as another. It just means that other lawyers may have particular experience that your attorney does not. Two heads are sometimes better than one, and sometimes having more attorneys involved in your case only makes your case stronger.

Assembling your team

As you probably already gathered, the investigation phase of your case is a team effort. It includes many different players. The first is your lawyer. Your lawyer will be directing your case. Your lawyer should have the expertise to know what kind of case you brought to him or her, what needs to be gathered, who needs to gather it, and who needs to be interviewed to determine what the case looks like. Think of your lawyer as the quarterback on the case. He's telling everyone where to go, how to go there, and what to do once they get there.

Your attorney may also have <u>paralegals</u> or <u>legal assistants</u> working to help organize your case. Paralegals and legal assistants are invaluable members of any legal team. They will often be responsible for collecting and organizing documents and information. They may even be a point of contact for you when your lawyer is not available. Paralegals and legal assistants will know what the case is about, what stage of investigation the case is at, and should be able to answer many of the questions that you may have about your case.

<u>Investigators</u> play a role on that team as well. As we know, investigators are the team members who are out in the field collecting more evidence—talking to witnesses, gathering documents, and seeing what the case looks like on the ground.

Your attorney may also employ <u>law clerks</u>, who are typically law students learning the business of practicing law. Law clerks can also be valuable members of the team. Law clerks will often be tasked with the business of researching particular issues that your case might present. Your lawyer will direct the law clerks in terms of the research they should do and the legal issues that might impact your case.

Because they are students and not practicing lawyers, law clerks often provide legal service without the sort of expense that comes with hiring another attorney. That is why your lawyer has them.

Since law students often come from a variety of different backgrounds before entering law school, they bring with them a variety of different experiences that even your attorney may not have. For example, I worked as a law clerk when I was in law school. I brought with me a decade of experience in the field of journalism. My experience as a journalist allowed me to bring an insight to cases that sometimes the lawyers I worked with did not have. I had knowledge about particular records that might exist out in the world and how to go about collecting those sorts of records. And I knew how to tell an effective story. The cases I was involved with often benefited from my experience, even if I did not walk into the case with a law degree and the sort of experience that the lawyer that I was working with had. While law clerks may not have the experience and the degree that your lawyer does, they are welcome members of the team that will be working on your behalf.

The last member of the team is you, the client. You will play a significant role in the investigation of your case, because you know the story of what happened to you better than anybody else. No matter how many years your attorney works on your case, no matter how many documents your attorney reads, no matter how many witnesses your attorney talks to, they will never know the story of what happened the way you do. That is why your involvement in your own case is of the utmost importance.

The last thing you want to do is simply hand your case over to an attorney and wait for something to happen. Be involved in your case. Give your lawyer ideas as to what sorts of records might exist, what sorts of medical records there might be, what sorts of witnesses need to be spoken to, and who those witnesses might be.

Your lawyer may even rely on you to make introductions to other people. An introduction from you could make them more comfortable talking to your lawyer about what happened, and giving your lawyer a better idea of what your case is all about. As you can imagine, most people do not care much for receiving a call from an attorney—it can often be an intimidating experience. A call from you to make an introduction can make all the difference in the world, reassuring those witnesses your attorney is just a human being wanting to ask a couple of questions.

Play an active role in your own case. Play an active role in the investigation. Do not sit back and assume that others will know about the answers that you already have. Talk to your lawyer. Talk to the other team members at your lawyer's office. Make notes, write a journal, and provide that material to your lawyer. With that information, your lawyer will be able to make your case as strong as it possibly can be.

How long will the investigation take?

The length of the investigative phase of your case will depend upon a number of factors. It will depend primarily upon how complex your case is. A simple auto accident may only take a week or two to investigate properly. A complex nursing home negligence case, however, may take months, even years, to determine how strong a case you have and whether or not you want to proceed. The time required may also depend upon the witnesses for your case, the location of your case, and the degree of cooperation your attorney receives from the agencies that possess your records. In short, it may take a while, so be patient.

Keep in touch with your attorney. Keep in touch with the team members that your attorney has working with him or her, but also keep in mind always that it may take some time in order to put your case together. Once the investigation is complete, both you and your attorney will have the opportunity to make a second determination as to one, whether you have a case, and two, what the strength of that case is. It will be important for you to sit down with your attorney when the investigation is completed, to make a determination of whether you want to move forward with your personal injury case or not.

When you sit down with your attorney at the end of the investigation, your attorney will be able to rely upon the information that the team has gathered, and apply to that information the law, your attorney's experience, and your attorney's expertise, to make a determination as to whether you can—and whether you want to—move on to the next phase of your personal injury case. You and your attorney together will decide whether you want to make a demand upon the person or corporation that caused your injuries.

Joe's Story

Investigator Dale Wilson got busy right away. He started with the police report, which gave him the name of the tractor trailer driver, Bill Buck, and showed that Bill was employed by Triple A Trucking. The report also listed two witnesses.

Dale spoke with the witnesses. He determined that a traffic camera had captured the incident on video, so he procured a copy of the video. He made sure that all the evidence of the crash was secured, including the vehicles, so that vehicles' black boxes could be collected. (Just like the black box in an airplane, the black box in newer autos collects all the information about what the vehicle was doing before the crash.)

In his investigation, Dale checked Bill Buck's record—not only his driving record but also looking to see if he had any criminal history that might be relevant. He also looked carefully at Triple A Trucking, since the company could possibly be responsible for Bill's actions, since Bill was actively working as their employee at the time of the crash.

Meanwhile, Jonathan's paralegal, Sara Garcia, was working to ensure that all the medical records, paramedic records, and police reports were collected. Sara also procured the coroner's report related to Mary's death, to determine the cause of her death, since the official cause of death could have some impact on whether there might be more than one party at fault. Jonathan and his team wanted to know whether there was any defect in the vehicles, or whether the incident was simply driver error. They also wanted to determine whether Mary might have had some kind of underlying health issues that contributed to her death, maybe something that made her more susceptible to the effect of the crash.

Once Jonathan and his team had completed their investigation on Joe's behalf, they were able to determine that there were no claims to be made against the truck manufacturer or the brake manufacturer or the manufacturer of Joe's vehicle. They looked to see who was responsible for the traffic light at the scene, and found that the light was owned and operated by the City of Denver. Since the city is protected by governmental immunity, it could not be held responsible for Joe's accident. They concluded that the only parties responsible for the accident were Bill Buck and Triple A Trucking.

Chapter Four

Making a Demand

IN CHAPTER TWO we talked about the three questions that would determine whether or not you have a case. Once you and your attorney have answered "yes" to those questions—that you in fact were harmed, that someone else was at fault, and that there is a value to be placed on the damages you incurred—and you have determined after an investigation that your case is worth pursuing, the next likely step is to prepare what lawyers call a demand letter.

A demand letter is the first attempt at telling your story to resolve your case. It is an attempt to get the other side to come to the table and make you whole without the expense and time of proceeding to full-blown litigation, and a trial. A demand letter is exactly what it sounds like: it is a letter, laying out the story of what happened to you, sent to either the person or corporation that caused your harm, or to their insurance company, along with a set of documents that support your claim.

Those documents that will support your claim are generally medical records. They could also be reports from experts. They may be video or audio recordings. And they may be photos of the accident itself, documenting your injuries and who you are. They are, essentially, the materials that will provide the support for your case in proving to the other side that you were harmed, and that the harm resulted from their negligence. The purpose of the demand letter is to convince the other side that having you pursue a lawsuit is not in their best interest.

A demand letter generally consists of three sections. The first section is the story of what happened and how it happened. That is the portion of the demand letter where much of the investigative work that you and your attorney have done will come into play. It will rely on your attorney's ability to tell the story of what happened to you.

The second portion of a demand letter is an explanation of how the at-fault party harmed you. In other words, it may not be enough for your attorney to simply say there was a car accident. It may require your attorney to explain how the at-fault party's actions caused that car accident, and once they caused that accident, show how it was that you were injured. That portion of the demand letter is often supported, again, with medical records and the conclusions of experts who have looked at the case to determine exactly why and how some accident did occur.

The third portion of any demand letter is an estimate of the damages that you have incurred as a result of the accident. Your damages estimate will be composed of two different kinds of damages, the first being economic damages. Economic damages are the sum of your medical bills and any out-of-pocket expenses that you may have incurred as a result of the accident. Economic damages may include time spent away from work where you did not receive a pay check. The economic damages may also include estimates for future medical care that you may need, or other costs that may be anticipated down the road.

The second portion of your damage estimate is what is referred to as non-economic damages—in other words, the things for which a price cannot be readily applied. How much pain have you experienced? How much suffering did you and your family and loved ones have to go through? How much inconvenience did you experience as a result of the at-fault party's actions? Non-economic damages will also include damages that are payable for physical disfigurement. In other words, was your body changed as a result of your particular accident? Did you suffer scarring? Did you lose a limb? Are you wheelchair-bound because your legs no longer work? Those sorts of damages are included in the assessment of non-economic damages. Your attorney will assign a value to those non-economic damages, add them to what you've determined are your economic damages, and then present one number that you believe encapsulates all of the harm that you have suffered.

The fourth and final part of any demand letter is the demand itself. Once you've laid out to the other side what happened, how it happened, and the resulting damages from that incident, your attorney will then make what is called a "demand" on the other side. A demand is a request for a particular amount of money that you, as the client, would be willing to walk away with without pursuing further litigation.

The amount of a demand will be based on a number of factors. The first, of course, is the strength of your case, in other words, how confident you and your attorney are that should you proceed to a lawsuit, you will in fact win that lawsuit. It will also depend on how badly you, as a client, need money now rather than two years from now. And finally, it will be based upon what you, as the client, are simply willing to walk away with. Determining that amount will require at least one discussion with your attorney so that you can arrive at that number as a team.

When making a demand, your attorney may not ask for your walk-away number right away. Your attorney may initially ask for a much higher number, with the idea that the number can be negotiated downward if need be.

But keep in mind that you, as a client, must have some input as to what that number will be. No one is in a better position than you to know exactly what it is that you will be satisfied with at the end of the day without having a day in court. So make sure to discuss that amount with your attorney when you are in the process of putting your demand letter together.

Typically, your attorney will draft the demand letter with the help of the team members involved in your case. That letter should then be shared with you, as the client, so that you can provide some input as well before it gets presented to the other side.

As a client, you will need to read the letter carefully to make sure it is factually accurate. You will also need to read the letter to ensure that it presents the sort of case that you want to present to the other side.

The timing of a demand letter is very important. You, as a client, must always remember that you've only got one shot at resolving your case, so you need to wait until you know the full extent of your injuries before taking any action. As the saying goes, you only get one trip to the well, so you better make sure you get a full bucket when you go. That same principle applies to your case. Only when you know the extent of your injuries, how long a recovery you are going to have, and how much money you will need to make you whole, should that demand letter be sent.

As a client, you may be anxious to get that letter out right away to get the process moving, but talk to your attorney about the best time to send the letter. It may require patience on your end.

Another factor that may help to determine when a demand letter needs to go out is the statute of limitations, as we discussed in Chapter 2. A statute of limitations is the limitation of time placed upon you by law for when you need to file a formal claim. Statutes of limitations vary from state to state and by type of claim, and you always must keep in mind that you need to file a lawsuit before the statute of limitations on your case runs out.

Should you find yourself at the end of your statute of limitations, your lawyer may determine that it is necessary to send out a demand letter without waiting to determine how severe your injuries might be. If your injuries and care are ongoing, and will be into the foreseeable future, you may be put in the position where you have to send out a demand letter and start talking about settlement without knowing the full extent of your injuries.

Should you and your attorney have to do that, it will be important for you to talk to your attorney about what those damages down the road might be. It will be important for your attorney to speak with your doctors about what your medical condition might be. And it may even be important to speak to an expert called a life care planner to make a determination as to how much your medical care over the course of the next several years—or even the rest of your life—may cost. And with that knowledge in mind you can reach out to the other side without waiting for the full extent of your injuries to be known, to see if your case can be resolved.

Once the letter is complete, and you and your attorney have agreed on the timing of the letter, your attorney will send the demand letter to a point of contact for the person or corporation who injured you. That may be an insurance company, another attorney, or possibly the at-fault party themselves.

Once that demand letter is sent out, everyone has to wait. The length of time you have to wait for a response may vary greatly depending upon your case.

Sometimes the people on the other side of your case have already had discussions amongst themselves about whether they want to settle, and how much they're willing to settle for. If that's the case, discussions could begin quickly. Other times, a demand letter will be received by someone who did not even know they were going to be sued. You may need to provide those individuals time to speak with an attorney, to speak with their insurance company, and possibly to do an investigation themselves.

It's important to note that sending out an initial demand letter is not necessarily the end of the process. You may be met with a flat-out denial of liability from the other side, or you may find that the other side wants to negotiate a settlement. That negotiation will often take the form of the other side sending a letter back, pointing out all the weaknesses in your case and pointing out all of the reasons that you are not injured as severely as you claim you are. Those sorts of letters can be frustrating to receive and to read. Make sure to talk to your attorney if you receive one of those letters so that your attorney can help you understand exactly what it means, and how you should proceed. Oftentimes, the other side will send letters like that simply to make you feel badly about your case and make you settle for less than what you're entitled to. It is important for you to talk to your attorney and rely on your attorney's experience and expertise in knowing whether the other side's letter is something to take seriously, or not.

Should you find yourself in a position where the other side wants to negotiate a resolution, be patient. Do not be the one who blinks first. Allow your attorney the necessary time to engage in good faith negotiations with the other side. Let your attorney see if a number can be agreed upon that would make you comfortable and make you whole going forward. As the process plays out, you may well find yourself with a number that does make you whole, and allows you to find justice for the harm that has been done to you. But the opposite may also occur. You may determine with your attorney that the other side does not want to resolve your case, or that they do not want to settle for an amount that will actually make you whole.

If that is the case, then you will move on to the next phase of your case: filing a lawsuit.

Joe's Story

In their initial meeting, Jonathan had made it clear to Joe that it would be best to wait until Joe's medical treatment was finished before they made a demand. But Joe's treatment could take a couple of years or more, and given the fact that Mary had died, they also needed to consider the statute of limitations for a wrongful death claim. In Colorado, the statute of limitations is two years from the date of the death.

So, Jonathan began compiling a demand letter for Joe's claim—both for his own injuries and for Mary's death. He started with Joe's medical bills. Joe incurred $25,000 as a result of his emergency room visit on the night of the accident and another $150,000 in subsequent medical bills, including treatment by his primary care doctor and an orthopedist. Joe will need to check in with his orthopedic doctor once a year for the next 10 years to make sure that the rods that were placed in his leg are doing the job properly. That will likely be another $10,000 over the next 10 years.

Next, Jonathan looked at Joe's lost wages. Joe missed two months of work from his job as the head mechanic for an automobile dealership. Based on his annual salary of $60,000, Joe lost $10,000 in wages. Jonathan then estimated Joe's non-economic damages at $200,000 for his pain and suffering, as well as his physical disfigurement. That brought the total demand for Joe's damages to $385,000.

Then Jonathan put together his figures for the wrongful death portion of the claim. The first was the loss of Mary's income. Mary had been a nurse with an annual salary of $60,000, and she was 42 years old when she died. Since she could have been expected to work another 20 years, her lost income was $1.2 million. Jonathan added in the non-economic damages—capped at $400,000 by Colorado law—and the $10,000 for funeral expenses. That brought the total for the wrongful death portion of the claim to $1,610,000.

On Joe's behalf, Jonathan sent a demand letter to the insurance carrier representing Bill Buck and Triple A Trucking, asking for a total of $2,995,000 for both Joe's damages and his wrongful death claim. The demand package also included supporting materials assembled by Jonathan's team. Then Joe and Jonathan sat back to wait for the insurance company's response.

ACT TWO:

DISCOVERY

Chapter Five

Filing a Lawsuit

AFTER YOU AND YOUR LAWYER have done all of the preliminary work, completed your investigation, and presented a demand, you may find that the other side is unwilling to resolve your case. That's when your case moves into what I describe as Act Two.

If your previous attempts to settle the case fail, either because the defendant simply does not want to settle or does not want to come up with enough money to settle, your only leverage at that point is to file a lawsuit and start moving toward a trial. In other words, you have two choices: you can drop your case altogether or you can make things official by filing suit in court.

Keep in mind that from the process of filing, onward through every step, nothing ever happens as quickly as it does on TV. We have all seen TV shows that portray the filing of a complaint and a trial that occurs two weeks later, with much drama in between. Nothing, unfortunately, could be further from the truth. Courts are, generally speaking, overworked, understaffed, and have far too many cases on their dockets. As a result, the process of moving from a complaint to a trial is a marathon not a sprint. It will take a long time. It is at least a matter of many months; sometimes it is a matter of years.

The process starts with the filing of a complaint. A complaint is a document that identifies the parties in the suit, that is, you and the person or corporation you are suing. In the complaint, you will be referred to as the plaintiff. The person or corporation you are suing will be known as the defendant.

The complaint relates the facts of your story and enumerates the legal claims that you are making against that other person or entity. The complaint does not have to contain every single detail of your case, and, in fact, courts don't want the complaint to do so. Generally, a judge wants to see in a complaint a short and concise version of what happened and what you are claiming as a result. That being said, the complaint does have to contain enough detail for the judge to say, assuming everything is true, that you have a claim and a jury should hear it. If you do not have that minimal level of detail in your complaint, the person you are suing can move to dismiss the complaint. Therefore, it is important to hit that middle ground—enough information to show that your claim is valid and not so much that you are writing a novel for the judge to sort through in order to determine whether or not you have a case.

One important decision you and your attorney will have to make is <u>where to file the complaint</u>. Generally, you have two options, either a state court or a federal court. Where you file your complaint will depend upon what the nature of the action is, in other words, what led to your injuries. Where your injury occurred will have some bearing on where you ultimately decide to file the complaint. Another deciding factor is where the parties are located. If you have a party that resides in another state, federal court may be your only option, but that is not always the case.

Once the complaint is filed, it is your responsibility to <u>have the complaint served on the other side</u>. Unlike most parts of this process, service is pretty close to what you see on TV. Someone shows up at the door, knocks on it, and when the other guy opens the door, the process server says "You've been served." It's not normally quite as dramatic as television would have you believe, but that is essentially how it works. You and your attorney have to ensure that the person or corporation you are suing gets a physical copy of the complaint.

There are, as always, some exceptions to that rule. If the defendant has a lawyer already, that lawyer may agree to waive service for you and allow you to simply send him a copy in the mail or via email. Then you file what's called a <u>waiver of service</u>, but it is just as valid as having the person knock on the door and serve the papers in person.

Once your defendant has that complaint, he or she has a deadline to respond to it and file what is called an <u>answer</u>. The answer is exactly what it sounds like. The answer is the defendant's version of events. It will state whether the defendant agrees with the events as you portrayed them. It will also serve as an opportunity for the defendant to establish the defenses that the defendant and the defendant's lawyer believe make the defendant either not liable at all, or liable for a smaller amount of money than what you are claiming.

The defendant's side usually has a few weeks in which to produce and serve the answer. Once the defendant does so, the case is considered to be <u>at issue</u>. At issue essentially means that the court now has jurisdiction over the claims and everybody can move forward with the many steps that follow a complaint, inching everyone closer to a trial.

One of the first things that both sides will need to do is share with each other what are called <u>disclosures</u>, meaning that the two sides exchange evidence and information that each considers relevant to the case. Disclosures are the information that each side possesses that is related to the claims thus far. Disclosures generally include documents that each side may possess that each believes are relevant to the claims and defenses. They will include names and contact information for any witnesses that the sides are aware of at the time. The plaintiff will have to provide a description of damages so that the defendant is on notice of what those damages may be. The defendant generally has to disclose insurance information as well.

Disclosure requirements vary depending on what court and what state in which you file. They are not uniform throughout the judicial system. Even in the same state, you might have two different rules of disclosure depending on whether you file in federal court or state court. So, it is very important to determine what the disclosure rules are for your particular case. Those rules will be found in either the state or federal rules of civil procedure. Those rules of civil procedure will dictate almost everything that conceivably may happen from the filing of the complaint all the way to presenting your case to a jury. They will contain your deadlines, the contents of motions, the manner in which the case must proceed, and things of that nature. The rules of civil procedure constitute the bible of procedure when it comes to prosecuting your claim in court.

One of the first things that the rules will dictate, regardless of where you are, is the scheduling conference with the court. A scheduling conference is the parties' opportunity to meet in advance and discuss scheduling items, including the amount of time for discovery, depositions (interviews under oath of the parties and witnesses), who can be deposed and for how long, how many documents can be exchanged, how many witnesses can be deposed and more. From that meeting the attorneys draft what is called a proposed scheduling order that is usually presented to the court for its approval. That scheduling order will provide a roadmap to both sides for how the case will proceed. It will set out deadlines for particular events, it will set out the limitations on discovery going forward; and sometimes it will contain an actual trial date, depending on what court you are in and what your court's preferences are.

Once the court approves the scheduling order, you have your roadmap for determining when everything is due and how the case will play out. It becomes your bible as your case goes forward.

Joe's Story

To no one's surprise, the insurance company refused Joe's claim. Instead, the company tried to pin the blame for the accident on Joe. Jonathan told Joe that his only recourse would be to file a lawsuit.

So Jonathan filed suit on Joe's behalf. The claims were simple. He brought a negligence claim against Bill Buck and Triple A Trucking, and a wrongful death claim against Mr. Buck and Triple A Trucking as a result of Mary's death.

Chapter Six:

Discovery

ONCE THE CASE is at issue, the first thing that both sides will do is engage in what is called discovery. Discovery is the period of time and process in which both sides get to learn all the information that they can about the other side's case and about their own case.

Written discovery

Attorneys can issue written discovery requests to which the other side has to respond. Written discovery requests are typically made up of three different elements: interrogatories, requests for admissions, and requests for documents.

Interrogatories are simply written questions that the other side needs to answer under oath. They can literally be any sort of question that is calculated to lead to the discovery of relevant evidence. Interrogatories can cover a wide expanse of information—everything from identifying information, to requesting the details of criminal histories, to asking specific questions about an incident, someone's injuries, or other things that the other side may have done during the course of litigation.

Interrogatories are usually made up of two different kinds, pattern interrogatories and standard interrogatories. Pattern interrogatories are questions that a court has previously drafted; they ask for baseline information; identification, driver's license information, insurance information, criminal history of the parties involved, and such. An attorney can simply cut and paste these pattern interrogatories into a request for information and the other side must answer.

Standard interrogatories, on the other hand, are any sort of question that you or your attorney want to ask of the other side for information that's relevant to the case. You can ask for a description of the events leading up to the accident: tell us what happened on the night of the car crash, or tell us what sorts of steps you took in order to avoid the accident. You can ask about witnesses that the other side has talked to—really, you can ask any sort of question that is designed to gather information about the case.

The court will limit you in regard to how many questions you can ask. If you have 40 questions and you're only allowed 20, you and your attorney will have to get creative and strategic to figure out which questions really need to be answered and which do not.

It is important to note that while interrogatories are designed to be answered by the other party under oath, most of the time the attorney on the other side is going to be drafting the answer, and as a result the answers to interrogatories are often not nearly as helpful as you would like them to be. Don't get frustrated. Your attorney knows how to deal with interrogatories and the answers to those interrogatories; your attorney will know how to harvest the good information from the other side's answers to use later when conducting depositions.

Requests for admissions are simple requests that ask the other side to admit to certain things. For example, you could ask the driver of the truck who ran into you to admit that he had not slept in over 24 hours before the accident. Or you could ask the truck driver's employer to admit that the driver was acting in the scope of his employment when the accident occurred. Like interrogatories, there are few rules that will dictate what or how you can ask for admissions. Getting straightforward answers, however, is sometimes another thing altogether.

Written discovery also includes requests for documents. In other words, you can ask the other side for actual physical documents that you believe exist, and that the other side possesses. These documents may be helpful to your case or at least give you a better idea as to what happened, who is liable, and what the damage are. Generally, that will allow you to ask for emails, correspondence, and memos related to the case. You can ask for medical records and police reports and other investigative materials from the other side. You can ask for insurance information and any other documents that you feel might be related to the case.

There are limitations on these requests for documents and interrogatories. The limitations will be created by the court and noted in the scheduling order. The court will set a number of requests that each side can make on the other. You won't be able to ask a hundred different questions or make a thousand different document requests. The judge will limit you to a particular number, and you will not get to ask more than that without showing good cause.

Once the document requests and interrogatories are all put together, your attorney will serve them on the other side. The other side will have a limited time in which to respond, usually about a month. When you and your attorney are satisfied that you have gotten all the information that you are going to get from these documents and interrogatories, you will proceed to conducting what are called depositions.

Depositions

Each side in the case has the opportunity to take depositions. Depositions are the first opportunity for your attorney to sit down with witnesses and opposing parties—under oath, with a court reporter present—and ask them questions face-to-face. It will be your first taste of what examining witnesses may look like at your trial.

Your attorney will use the opportunity to take depositions to: 1) gather more information about the case, and 2) assess how the witnesses and the parties in the case will testify and present in front of a jury. Your attorney will be watching carefully, observing the witnesses' behavior, how they answer questions, and how they react under the stress of questioning.

Any time you are taking a deposition of a witness or a party from the other side, your attorney is going to be assessing how that witness is going to present to a jury. How will that witness ultimately affect your case? We often look at what a witness has written in a police report and think that witness is really going to hurt us going forward, but when given the opportunity to sit down and question that witness about their opinions or about their observations, we find that our initial impressions were wrong. We may find that the witness in fact did not see everything that they thought they saw, that things are not as crystal clear in the witness' mind as the witness thought they were, or that the witness is simply just not confident about what the witness saw or heard. As a result, we may find that the witness's testimony is much weaker than we originally anticipated, thus making your case stronger.

The opposite, of course, can also hold true. Sometimes a witness you thought was not going to play much of a role in your case could turn out to be absolutely key. Your attorney may ask questions of that witness and determine that they in fact know much more than you thought they did, or that they are going to present to a jury much better than you thought they would. In that case, your case may become weaker, because that witness's testimony will be considered more credible or more detailed than you originally thought.

One of the most important things your attorney will want to do in any deposition is see how a witness deals with difficult questions. Does that witness get rattled, or does that witness stay calm the entire time? I recall a witness I deposed many years ago. I was barely out of the gate, simply asking who he was and where he lived, and it took no more than two more questions for the witness to get up out of his chair and challenge me to a fight.

He was an opposing witness. At one point he had brought up an issue about how he had been counseled by the other side's attorney on how he was dressed. So I simply asked him during the course of the deposition, "What advice were you given about how to dress?" He took great offense at that and asked why in the world he would need to be counseled on how to dress. Didn't he dress fine already? And asking me, shouting at me from across the table, he stood up and began to walk around the table toward me and threatened to fight me.

We took a brief break. I did not ask many more questions after that. I didn't need to—I knew as a result of that deposition that the witness was clearly someone with a short temper who was not going to do well under cross-examination at trial. So instead of giving him more preparation for what was in store, we called the deposition early and dealt with the small amount of information we had.

On another occasion, we had just the opposite result. I had a witness statement from a particular witness with very little detail and a seemingly inconsistent recounting of exactly what happened. When we had a chance to depose her, she was able to give a very specific recollection of exactly what happened and give us a very good description as to why her written statement was the way it was. She ended up being a much stronger witness for the other side than we ever anticipated she would be. Her testimony hurt. As a result of her testimony, we ended up settling the case for a less money than we originally anticipated the case was worth.

In the end, your attorney will assess the reliability of the information that each witness and party may be providing, and ultimately determine how those witnesses might appear to a jury. Based on those assessments, your attorney will continue to determine how strong your case is or where the weaknesses in your case might be, and will continue to develop your case around those witnesses.

As a party to the case, you have the right to be present at every deposition. Your presence may help. You may be able to assist your attorney regarding the subjects the attorney is asking about. Your mere presence may help to keep the witness honest. But the opposite can also be true. Your presence may prohibit an open and honest exchange with the witness. It will all depend on the circumstances.

Be sure to have a conversation with your lawyer about whether or not you should be in the room.

Expert disclosures

The fourth element of discovery that will take place is that of <u>expert disclosures</u>. Experts, as we know, are people hired to provide opinions in your case that a lay person simply cannot supply on their own. Usually those witnesses are doctors, engineers, life care planners, economists, or other people with some specific education or background that enables them to look at a set of facts and provide opinions based upon their education, background, or experience. These experts may form opinions as to causation, the extent of injuries, the value of lost work and wages, life care needs, and a multitude of other subjects.

Each side has the responsibility of disclosing detailed information about any expert witness they plan to use in the case going forward. The rules will require both sides to provide a detailed accounting of each expert's opinion, usually in the form of an <u>expert report</u>. The expert report will contain the entirety of the expert witnesses' opinions and the basis for those opinions.

Your attorney will also have to provide the other side with your witnesses' professional history and background, usually in the form of a resume. Each side will have to tell the other how much money they are paying their experts to provide opinions in the case and each will have to provide a listing of the experts' testimony from past cases. With all that information, most of the time your attorney will then want to depose the other side's expert witnesses, and from those depositions make the same sorts of assessments that your attorney would make with any other witness.

It is important to keep in mind that any time an expert witness is involved in your case it will be expensive. You will have to pay for your own expert witnesses' time, and when you choose to depose the other side's expert witnesses you'll have to pay for their time as well. Depending on the expert and the extent of their testimony, that can get expensive. So, make sure you talk to your attorney during the course of discovery and make good decisions about who to depose and how long to depose them, because even though your attorney may be supplying the cost for those witnesses up front, ultimately you, as the client, will be responsible for paying them.

Your attorney will assess expert witnesses in the same way as any other witness, considering both the information the expert is offering and the way the expert is likely to be perceived by a jury. Oftentimes on paper an expert witness will look very good. The expert will have a very good educational background, lots of experience that they can write about, and a detailed opinion that appears to put your case to bed. But upon deposing that witness your attorney may realize there are giant gaping holes in that witness' testimony. Perhaps the manner in which the expert went about forming his or her opinion is simply unreliable or is guesswork. Perhaps it is an opinion that any lay person could have come to on their own. In those cases your attorney can exploit the experts' weaknesses, and possibly even get the witness barred from testifying at all.

But again, the opposite can also hold true. An expert witness who seemingly has only a little bit of experience or a small amount of education or experience in the subject matter at hand may prove to have a very reliable opinion in the matter. It may be backed up by scientific evidence and principles and make for a very strong and damaging opinion.

I recall taking the deposition of a witness in a case who was testifying regarding the level of intoxication of a group of people. On paper, this witness had a great deal of experience in the field and outstanding credentials from a variety of different educational institutions. However, when we finally sat down to depose that witness, we found she was basing her opinion purely upon the observations of people who were present at the scene. Her opinion had nothing to do with science nor did it in any way rely upon her expertise. It simply relied upon the observations of other people who happened to be there. Her degrees and her experience were simply window dressing for what she was asked to say. As a result of doing that deposition, the other side chose to not call her as a witness at trial. It did significant damage to their defense.

Your deposition

Ultimately the other side is going to want to take your deposition. That is often the most stressful part of the discovery process for any person who has filed a lawsuit. Put simply, it's just scary. Most of the time, it will be your first experience of being cross-examined by an attorney. And it will be accomplished with every word that you say being taken down by a court reporter, and forever memorialized on paper.

Here is the good news: Your attorney understands that it is a scary proposition and will make sure you are ready. Your attorney will prepare you thoroughly for that deposition, so do not stay awake at night worrying about it. In working with you to prepare, your attorney will make the same evaluations of you that he or she does of any other witness. Your attorney will evaluate you on how credibly you come across, the quality of information that you would present to a jury, and whether or not you would appear likable to a jury. Your attorney will help you answer tough questions to make you more comfortable with the information, and with the process, before you actually sit down at that table and begin to answer questions from the other side.

Generally speaking, I give every client three different rules to abide by before they go into a deposition. The first rule is be honest. In your case the truth is your best weapon against the other side, so don't feel the need to embellish or hide facts along the way. If a question is presented to you and you have an answer, give that answer.

The second rule is listen to the questions that is being presented to you and answer only that question. In other words, do not volunteer information. Listen very closely to exactly what the attorney is asking you to answer, answer the question in as few words as you can, and then stop.

It is human nature to want to explain everything. It is human nature to want to have a conversation, and give details, and explain why you did something or why you did not do something. Your deposition is not one of those opportunities. The attorney on the other side wants you to provide more information. The attorney wants you to keep talking so that they can discover more information about you and about the case that the other side is not necessarily entitled to.

There have been occasions during my life as a lawyer where clients have ignored this advice and not stopped talking. They tried to explain everything away because they truly believed in their heart that they had an answer and an explanation for everything. I can tell you that 100 percent of the time those clients have hurt their case along the way. Why? Because they open doors to information that is not relevant to the case. Those clients simply gave the other side the ability to ask about that information, kept themselves in the hot seat longer, and got worn out in the process. Do not be that client. Listen to the question and answer that question, then stop.

The third rule is take a deep breath and relax. Your attorney will be at your side during the entire course of the deposition. Your attorney will be there to protect you, to object to questions that are objectionable, and to ask for a break when you need one. There is no reason to think that you will be there on your own. You will be there as part of a team and you will have someone watching your back.

Once we have a date for your deposition, we will set another date with you to come into the office to talk about the case. That meeting will usually last a minimum of several hours, because we will put you through the questions that we anticipate the other side is going to ask.

The object of this meeting is not to craft your answer to be something different from the truth, but simply to make sure that you can articulate the answers to those questions. By asking you questions for several hours, we will also try to simulate what it will be like to be in a deposition. We want it to be tedious and boring. We want you to get tired along the way. Experience is the best preparation we can give you.

There will be a point where you simply do not want to answer any more questions, but under the rules and under the law you will have to keep going until the lawyer on the other side is out of questions, or the allotted time is used up—usually seven to eight hours. Our goal is to get you used to that feeling, so that when the feeling ultimately arrives during the course of your deposition you already know what it feels like.

We will also make assessments as to how you present yourself while answering those questions. Are you looking people in the eye when you are answering questions or are you looking down at your lap? Are you confident in the truth of your answers? Are you simple and straightforward in the manner in which you go about answering questions? These are important assessments to make, because we know the other side is going to make the same assessments about you and therefore the strength of your case. The better the impression you make on the other side, the stronger your case becomes.

Sometimes after that first meeting we will determine that you need another opportunity to prepare. Sometimes we will determine you need two more opportunities, or even three more, and we will take all of those opportunities to ensure that you are fully prepared as best you can be. When it comes to your deposition you only get one shot, and we want to make sure that shot is as good as it can possibly be.

While driving to your lawyer's office over and over again to answer questions about the case—questions you have answered a hundred times before—may seem tedious and boring, it is an incredibly important part of your preparation for your case, so make sure you make the time available for that preparation to happen.

Every client is different. Every client has different experience in public speaking and presenting themselves and answering questions under oath. Some clients can come in for a single session of preparation and be ready to go. Others need far more preparation.

I recall one witness in particular who was very uncomfortable with answering questions about the incident. It was a medical malpractice case, so she was talking about personal medical issues. These were things that were very personal to her, and quite frankly things that were embarrassing. It made a difficult job that much harder for her. But by simply taking the time to talk about those issues, making her comfortable with talking about them, we enabled her to sit down and answer questions about her injuries and what happened, even though the answers to those questions were the very last thing in the world she wanted to discuss.

We brought her in on four different occasions to prepare her prior to her actual deposition taking place. It ended up being far more time than I have ever spent with any witness prior to their deposition testimony, but it paid off in spades. By the time we got to her deposition she was comfortable with the questions, and she was comfortable with the truth of the answers to those questions, such that she could sit in that chair for eight hours and answer every question the other side's attorney threw at her. She did so confidently and articulately. And as a result of her performance, we were able to resolve her case a short time later.

Summary judgment

After your deposition, there may be one last hurdle through which to jump before you go to trial. That is summary judgment. Generally speaking, when discovery is completed—when all the interrogatories have been answered, all the documents have been produced, and all the depositions have been completed—both sides will have an opportunity to present to the court motions for summary judgment. A motion for summary judgment, usually presented by the defendant, essentially says to the court that, based on all the evidence as it exists right now, you the plaintiff are not able to win because the law precludes you from winning on this particular claim. Should the defendant file such a motion, your only goal is to get beyond that motion for summary judgment and have the court declare that there is some issue of fact that a jury needs to decide.

If there is a motion for summary judgment, the court will look at the evidence that both sides have gathered during the course of discovery, and the court may then say that as a matter of law you cannot win, and there is no sense in presenting this case to a jury. Obviously, such a ruling would be devastating. So the stakes in a motion for summary judgment are very high.

Should a court grant the other side's motion for summary judgment, your case may end then and there. You may find yourself with the painstaking decision of whether to spend years appealing that decision or simply drop your case altogether. That is why a ruling on a summary judgment motion can be so significant. But if we've done our job right along the way, we should have enough facts and evidence to present to the court to say, "There is a valid claim here, and a jury should decide it going forward."

In my experience, summary judgment doesn't occur very often. Normally, a court will look at the evidence presented and find some factual issue that a jury is going to have to decide. However, that being said, if the court doesn't find that factual issue, or decides as a matter of law that you simply cannot win, the effects on your case can be devastating. I was involved in one case that was dismissed at the summary judgment stage, a matter of weeks prior to the case going to trial. As a result of the court's granting of that motion, the case spent the next five years in appeals before it was ultimately sent back down for a trial. Those were five years the family was forced to spend its own funds, countless time, and herculean effort caring for a loved one 24 hours a day, all while wondering if they would ever achieve justice. Fortunately, they did. But it was a wait and a fight that I would not wish upon anyone.

Joe's Story

In discovery, Jonathan sent out interrogatories to Bill Buck and Triple A Trucking. He asked about Mr. Buck's version of events, his driving history, and his criminal history. He requested documents from Triple A Trucking, including Bill Buck's personnel file, his driver logs, any internal company emails or memoranda about the crash, maintenance records for the truck involved in the crash, and copies of any dash cam video from the truck that captured the events leading up to the crash.

Jonathan decided to depose both Bill Buck and a representative of Triple A Trucking. He wanted to hear Bill's detailed description of how and why the crash occurred. Jonathan wanted to hear from both Bill and the trucking company about the maintenance of the truck, including any work that had been done or needed to be done on the truck immediately before the accident. He also wanted to get a detailed description of the results of any investigation performed by AAA Trucking after the accident.

Bill Buck's version of the events was just the opposite of Joe's. Bill claimed that he had a green light at the time of the accident, and that Joe had run the red light, making it impossible for Bill to avoid the collision. But the dash cam video from the truck showed that Bill Buck's light had just turned red before he drove through the intersection. Bill had gambled on the yellow light.

Despite the evidence produced in discovery, Triple A Trucking and Bill Buck still weren't willing to take responsibility for the accident, so they forced Joe to take them to trial.

ACT THREE:

TRIAL

Chapter Seven

Going to Court

THE TIME HAS COME. All of your efforts at settlement have failed. That means your case has entered its third act, going to trial. This is truly the only leverage remaining, literally your only shot to be made whole for the harms and injuries that you've suffered as a result of whatever kind of incident you were involved in.

Civil case vs. criminal case

A personal injury case is a civil case, not a criminal case. Why is that distinction important? There are some significant differences between civil and criminal cases. Again, neither is like what you have seen on TV or in the movies, and it is worth taking a moment to distinguish between the two.

A civil case differs from a criminal case in several very important ways. The first difference is in what we call the burden of proof. In any criminal case, the burden of proof on the prosecutor is to prove their case beyond a reasonable doubt, which is the highest burden that our justice system places on any litigant. It is a very high standard that a prosecutor has to meet in order to prove that someone committed a crime.

The burden of proof in a civil case is preponderance of the evidence. That means your burden is to prove only that you are more likely right than wrong. I've seen many different analogies used to describe what a preponderance of the evidence is. This is the one I think most appropriate: Imagine that you are holding 50 sheets of paper in each hand. If you were to take one more sheet of paper and put it on your left hand, your left hand would hold a preponderance of the evidence. In other words, one more sheet, just a little bit more. The burden of proof in a civil case therefore is much lower than it is in a criminal case. It is just a matter of proving that you are more likely right than the other side is.

In a civil case, like yours, there is no prosecutor. It's just you and your attorney or attorneys proving your case. When the trial is finished and the jury comes back and delivers its verdict, no one is going to go to jail regardless of what that verdict states. The only thing a civil jury is empowered to do is determine liability and award you money as a result. While it may seem crass, money is the only mechanism by which a jury in a civil case makes things right.

The jury will have three questions presented to them at the end of the trial that they will have to answer. The issues may seem complicated as presented to the jury, but in essence they boil down to three questions. The first: Is there liability? In other words, was the person who harmed you negligent or something more than negligent? And if the answer to that first question is yes—the other person or corporation acted negligently, and you and your attorney have proved that question by a preponderance of the evidence—the jury answers the second question: What are the damages? There can be many parts to the damages question, taking into account the various economic and non-economic damages you may have suffered, but in the end those numbers are all totaled up to determine what your total damages are. Then the jury answers the third and final question by determining whether the defendant's negligence caused your injuries.

If the jury determines the defendant was negligent, that you suffered damages, and that the defendant caused those damages, the jury issues a verdict for a particular amount of money. The verdict sends no one to prison, it simply orders the other side to pay up.

The Trial

On the first day of trial, the judge begins by taking care of any preliminary matters that your attorney feels are necessary. Then it is on to the first step in the actual trial process—jury selection. That is assuming you have not chosen a bench trial, in which the judge is the sole person who decides everything from liability to damages. For purposes of this discussion, let's assume you have chosen a jury, the choice that most litigants make.

Step One: Jury Selection

Jury selection is just what it sounds like. You and your attorney get to choose, along with the defendant's team, a jury that will hear your case. That decision-making process begins by calling a panel of jurors. In other words, the judge will bring in more jurors than are necessary to hear your case. An initial panel may consist of anywhere from 12 to 30 jurors (and maybe more), from whom the appropriate number of jurors will be selected. The number of jurors you will be entitled to may be 6, 8, 10 or even 12; it will vary depending on the state and the court you are in.

The goal of the system in choosing a jury is to find an impartial group of people—citizens and community members—who can listen to the evidence and apply the law to the facts as directed by the judge. In reality, when it comes to jury selection, your goal, and your attorney's goal, is to find those jurors who are already set against you (your enemies), and get rid of those jurors. Get them off the panel so that they will not hear your case.

Obviously, that begs the question: How do you know which jurors are your enemies? You do that by asking the jurors questions and starting conversations with them and among them—finding out a little bit about who they are. The legal term for the process is *voir dire*, a French term that means "to speak the truth." (The literal meaning of the French for all the Francophiles reading this is "to see to speak.") Again, depending on the jurisdiction, the time allotted for voir dire will vary greatly. Sometimes you will get a matter of minutes, sometimes a matter of hours, and in some places a matter of days.

The process normally starts with the judge, who will do some initial questioning of every juror on the panel in terms of the jurors' background, their family, their education, where they live, what they do for a living, and things of that nature.

Once that initial round of dry questioning is done, and each juror has answered those basic questions, the lawyers may then have the opportunity to ask questions of their own. The questions that lawyers ask of jurors tend to be more specific. They will dig a little deeper, beyond the identifying information of each juror. The lawyers will ask about jurors' beliefs, their biases, things that have happened in their lives, their political beliefs, and other issues that may affect their ability to listen to your case and find in your favor.

When asking those questions, your lawyer's goal is simply to find your enemies. Your lawyer wants to find out who is not going to rule in your favor, no matter how good your evidence is, and get them off of your jury. Officially, the goal is to excuse them from the jury box.

Excusing jurors is done through what we call strikes. There are two different kinds of strikes: strikes "for cause" and peremptory strikes. A judge may strike a juror for cause because that juror has indicated they are so dead set in their beliefs or biases that they simply could not listen to the evidence in the case and make an impartial determination.

Strikes for cause can sometimes happen, for instance, when a doctor is being asked to pass judgment on another doctor. It can happen because political beliefs or religious beliefs prohibit a juror from finding in a particular way. It is very difficult to excuse a juror for cause, but when the grounds arise, it becomes your lawyer's obligation to request from the judge that the juror be stricken for cause (and the judge's obligation to strike them), for the reasons that the juror has described.

For example, we had an individual on an accident case, who when asked about the law and the burden of proof, said he didn't think he could comply with that law. We asked him why. He was clearly the type of individual who simply did not want to serve on a jury in the first place. He dug deep into the recesses of his memory and came up with a philosophical reason, from a philosopher that he had read about in college. He declared that based upon the philosophy of that particular philosopher (whose name escapes me today) he could not sit on a jury and apply the law. He believed that universal law as that philosopher had described, and not as the court would have it, was a better measure of whether or not someone should be held liable for someone else's injuries. As a result, he could not change his beliefs in any way, shape, or form to comport with what the judge was asking him to do. Because of that, we asked the judge for a strike for cause. It was granted.

Challenges for cause are limitless; there is no fixed number that the attorneys can use during the course of jury selection. But finding the appropriate grounds to excuse a juror for cause is rare. As a result, you will not likely see it happen in your case.

The other kind of strike that your lawyer can use is a <u>peremptory</u> <u>strike</u>. A preemptory strike can be used against a juror for any reason at all, so long as that reason is not based on race or some other protected class. So, peremptory strikes are your lawyer's opportunity to strike jurors that they or you just do not like; that everyone just gets a bad feeling about. If a juror says something during those conversations that strikes you the wrong way, that indicates to you that they might not be a good fit, you can get rid of him. If a juror gives you a weird look during the course of jury selection, or makes you uncomfortable, you can get rid of him. If a juror is wearing an Iron Maiden t-shirt, and the bad time you had at an Iron Maiden concert in college makes you nervous about the juror, you can get rid of him.

Who are the jurors I try to excuse? On every jury panel there are people who believe there are too many lawsuits in this country and that the legal system is out of control. They have usually watched too much news, or too much television, and determined that the judicial system is the problem. Those sorts of jurors are probably not going to find in your favor, and I will usually try to get rid of them when they pop up. The obvious problem with that is sometimes there are more jurors like that on a panel than we have peremptory strikes. When that happens, our best bet is to get rid of as many of them as we can and hope that the jurors remaining on the panel are able to listen to the evidence and see that perhaps they were wrong about their initial impressions of the judicial system.

You should plan to lose jurors you like along the way. The jurors who come to mind are the ones that I really want and that the other side ends up striking. For example, in a recent medical malpractice trial we tried, there was a juror who seemed to like us very much. She continued looking over at our table, and looking at me, and smiling at us, and smiling at my client, and just engaging nonverbally. We thought, "That juror looks great. She's already engaged, she's already indicating to us that she likes us." So we really hoped that she remained on the panel. We did everything we could to hide her from the other side. Unfortunately, the lawyer on the other side also noticed her nonverbal communication. He noticed that she was looking at my client and smiling at all of us, so he decided that she might be bad for his case. She was the first juror that he used a peremptory strike to dismiss.

The peremptory strike can be used for almost any reason. The caveat is that the number of peremptory strikes is limited, based upon number of jurors in the initial panel, and the number of jurors ultimately needed for the case.

There are two ways in which it normally works: one is that a piece of paper is passed back and forth between your lawyer and the other side's lawyer. Each side has an opportunity to cross out one name. And when enough names are crossed out so that the remaining names add up to the total number of jurors needed, you've got a jury. The other is when each side stands and orally dismisses a particular juror, again, until the panel is reduced to only the number of jurors needed.

Those jurors remaining will be the group of people who sit in the jury box, listen to the evidence, and decide your case. The judge will excuse all those jurors who have been stricken by both sides. Then he swears in your jury, they take the oath, and the jury gets ready to hear the evidence.

Step Two: Opening Statements

Once your jury has been selected and sworn in, the lawyers will make their opening statements. The plaintiff's attorney always goes first—your attorney—and the defendant's attorney follows.

This is usually the jurors' first opportunity to hear your side of the case. It is your lawyer's opportunity to tell the story of what happened—to tell the story of what the defendant did to you and the story of how your life has been affected because of the defendant's actions. It is a preview of the evidence that is going to be presented during the course of the trial.

It is important to note that this is not an argument. These are not known as opening arguments; they are opening statements. Argument is actually prohibited by the judge at this point in the trial. Oftentimes the judge will admonish both lawyers before opening statements begin, warning them not to argue.

In its purest form, the opening statement is just a matter of storytelling. Your lawyer will stand before the jury and walk them through everything that occurred. Some lawyers are more skilled at this than others. You will be able to tell pretty quickly how much skill each lawyer has in doing so.

Everyone is familiar with storytelling. We hear stories growing up. We read them in books. We watch them in movies. We listen to them on the radio. The story that a lawyer tells during the opening statement is no different. As you listen to the opening statements, based on your experience alone, you should be able to determine who the better storyteller in the room is. Obviously, you want the better storyteller on your side. During the course of opening statements, you will be able to tell by watching the jurors just how engaged they actually are. Are they leaning forward? Are they nodding along? Are they actually paying attention to what the lawyer is saying? Sometimes they are and sometimes they're not. Hopefully, they're paying attention to your lawyer and not paying attention to the other.

In addition to storytelling, the lawyers are going to show some of the evidence in the case. They may have an opportunity to show documents, show video of what happened, and show photographs of the scene. They will have an opportunity to show the jury how the accident or injury has affected your life.

The decision of what goes into an opening statement is a strategic one. It is perhaps one of the most important decisions that we make prior to going into a trial. As a lawyer, I have to determine what information is necessary to tell the story of what happened and to tell what the defendant did, within the very limited amount of time allotted to do so. Rarely does a judge allow lawyers carte blanche to use as much time as they want. The judge normally places time limits upon each attorney and the attorney is not allowed to go over that time. So, when giving an opening statement, the lawyer is not able to simply regurgitate everything under the sun that has occurred.

Therefore, when I prepare an opening statement, it becomes important for me to economize my words and determine what is truly important and what is not. Usually the story becomes better having gone through that editing process. It becomes a story that jurors will understand, and will be interested in hearing more of.

It is important for your lawyer, during an opening statement, to talk about any weaknesses in your case. That may seem strange. Why would your lawyer talk about the kinds of things that only help the defendant? It is important that your lawyer brings up the facts that hurt your case, and addresses them at the outset, because the defendant's attorney will almost certainly talk about them. Because the jury will inevitably hear about those "bad facts," it becomes important that each juror hears them from your lawyer, to avoid the appearance that you are trying to hide anything. If there is a perceived or potential weakness in the case, get it out in the open and tell the jurors why it is simply not important. Explain why it will not affect their decision at the end of the day. By doing so, your lawyer is able to blunt the veiled arguments that the defense lawyer is going to make once that lawyer stands up and starts his or her opening statement. And if the jury already knows about those facts, the defense lawyer gets little reaction when he or she raises the issue anew.

Bringing up bad facts also grants credibility to your side. And credibility is at the very heart of persuasion.

That means part of crafting an opening statement is trying to make a determination in our own minds what the defense is going to find important. What facts work against us? Sometimes we end up being more conservative than we have to be and talk about more bad facts than are necessary, because it turns out the defense did not believe that those facts were important enough to raise them. But in these circumstances it is generally better to be overly cautious, because we never want the defense to be the first side to talk about any bad facts.

Lawyers have won or lost cases simply because of their opening statements. Obviously, you are not going to know it at the time, but a juror might tell you that at the end of the trial. That is why your attorney will spend a great deal of time preparing for the opening statement, to make sure that statement is as good as it possibly can be. The opening statement needs to be engaging, compelling, and believable, so that the jury simply knows when your lawyer sits down that you have already won. You want each juror to be convinced that your case is just and that they need to make things right.

Let me give you an example from a recent case. My client had been injured in a horrific automobile accident. In the opening statement, we walked through all of the necessary elements and got to the point where we were describing to the jury how the accident had affected my client's life. And those effects were significant. We were telling the story of a girl who had been an athlete and a fantastic student and was now going to be bedridden and wheelchair-bound literally for the rest of her life—maybe another 30 or 40 years. She needs round-the-clock care and is unable to do anything for herself. When we got to the end of that opening statement, two of the jurors had tears running down their faces because of their understanding of what had happened to this girl.

So when we got done with that, we had a pretty good idea that things were going in the right direction. We knew at that point we had at least two jurors who understood, who empathized with the position of our client, and who might argue in our favor to the other jurors. It was a good feeling.

I have to admit that the opposite has also happened. During the course of an opening statement, I once had a juror fall asleep and simply stop paying attention at all to what was going on. In addition to being a blow to my ego (as a lawyer, I presume that everybody wants to hear everything that I have to say), it also indicated to us that perhaps the story we were telling and the manner in which we were telling that story was not as compelling as we thought it was. As a result, we made some changes in the way we were going to tell the story throughout the rest of the trial, and things worked out okay. But it certainly was not the reaction we were hoping for.

In general, as a plaintiff's attorney, we want to see more tears than we do people falling asleep. That's generally a sign that things are going better than worse.

The opening statement from the defendant's attorney is obviously a very good opportunity to determine exactly what the defense in the case is going to be and how it is going to be portrayed. But normally there are no big surprises. It is simply a matter of a defense attorney choosing from two or three defenses that the defense could present and determining which one, in the defendant's mind, is the most important. There have been times where we did not know exactly how the defense was going to go about defending the case, or what they were going to bring up along the way, so to some degree, it can affect how we approach the remainder of the trial. But we are rarely surprised to the point where we have to blow up our case and make radical changes along the way.

The opening statement given by your lawyer can often be very encouraging to you as the plaintiff. You will likely feel good having heard your lawyer stand up, tell the story of what happened and how you have been harmed. It will be reassuring to hear that in a short time, the jurors will be asked to find in your favor. Beware, though, that the opposite is true with the defendant's opening statement. The defendant's story can be a difficult story to hear, because the defendant's lawyer will talk about every weakness in your case. The lawyer will talk about everything that you did wrong along the way. The lawyer will talk about everything that is bad about your case. It is very easy at the end of the defendant's opening statement, just shortly after feeling on top of the world after your own opening statement, to feel like things are going very badly.

But have heart. The jurors have already listened to your lawyer tell the story from your perspective. The ability to go first is a very powerful tool to have in your belt. Why? Because once jurors make their minds up about something—once they determine that something is true—it is very difficult to change their minds, no matter how good the defendant's opening statement might be. It is basic human psychology. So keep that knowledge in your back pocket, and have faith that things have gone well through opening statements as you move into the next phase of the trial.

Step Three: Presentation of Witnesses

Once we are done with opening statements, you, as the plaintiff, get to present your witnesses and your evidence. This is what is known as your case-in-chief. You get to go first. This is the opportunity for your lawyer to put the evidence in your case in front of the jury so that they can hear the witnesses, they can look at the pictures, they can see the video, and then make a determination of what the truth is and whether that truth falls in your favor or not.

The first way we do that is through something called <u>direct examination</u>. Direct examination is what happens when we ask questions of friendly witnesses, in other words, witnesses that we want to present. The lawyer will ask open-ended questions that start with who, what, when, why, where, and how. The witness will have the opportunity to answer those questions, elaborate on answers, and simply have a conversation with your lawyer. Most of the time you will find that direct examinations are conversational in style; they are developed to give the witness the opportunity to tell the story of what happened through the witness's eyes.

Through those witnesses your lawyer can also introduce <u>evidence</u>. You will see that your lawyer will introduce pictures, documents, and maybe even video that a witness may have made along the way. Your attorney will use the opportunity of direct examination to introduce those exhibits into evidence, in other words, make them a part of the official record of the case. Once something becomes evidence, the jurors are able to take it back to the jury room with them at the end of the day to review it again. Things that do not become evidence do not become part of the official court record and the jury is not able to review those things while they are deliberating. It is important during the course of direct examination for your lawyer to move into evidence all those things that are truly important for the jury to have when they go back to the deliberation room at the end of the trial.

Keep in mind that your attorney may not introduce everything that you have. Your attorney does not necessarily want to present to the jury every single document, photograph, and piece of video that may exist. The presentation of evidence is, like everything else in a trial, strategic. Your lawyer will want to economize what things the lawyer sends back and what the lawyer does not. What no lawyer wants is to overwhelm a jury with too many documents and too many photos. Doing so can simply confuse the issues. Some of the best advice that can be given to any attorney is to keep it simple so that the jury knows exactly what exhibit to look for or picture to look at when the jury is trying to answer the questions that the judge ultimately provides.

Another strategic element of your case worthy of thought will be the order of the witnesses that your lawyer presents for direct examination. Your lawyer will work out how your story will best be told through the presentation of various witnesses. Generally, that will be broken down into specific chapters. Those chapters will include what actually happened in the incident, then the injuries you have suffered, and how those injuries may have affected you going forward. Eye witnesses may testify about what happened and how you were injured. Doctors may testify about how those injuries will affect you for the rest of your life. All of that information will come out through a variety of witnesses—both lay witnesses and expert witnesses—that you and your lawyer have decided to present to tell your story.

When your lawyer is done examining each witness, that witness will then be subject to cross-examination. Cross-examination is the stuff of movies. Cross-examination is that moment in A Few Good Men when Tom Cruise yells at Jack Nicholson, "I want the truth!" Rarely does it get that dramatic in real life, but cross-examination usually provides the most dramatic moments of any trial. It is the opportunity for one side of the case to question the opposing side's witness and to poke holes in that witness's story. The opposing lawyer will poke holes in the witness's credibility and possibly poke holes in everything that the witness has said or done.

Normally a lawyer will not ask a question during the course of cross-examination to which the lawyer does not already know the answer. Lawyers know those answers because they know the exhibits, they know the evidence, and they have deposed the witnesses. Your lawyer will already know exactly what each witness is going to say.

In direct examination, the lawyers can only ask open-ended questions. But in cross-examination, the lawyers will ask what are called leading questions. Leading questions already contain the answer that the lawyer wants.

A leading question, instead of starting out with who, what, when, why, where or how, begins with a statement. Instead of saying, "How fast were you going?" the lawyer will say, "You were going 75 miles an hour, weren't you?" Instead of saying, "Were you able to see the whole thing?" the lawyer is going to say, "You weren't able to see the whole thing because a large truck was in front of you blocking your view, wasn't it?"

In TV shows and movies, it is common to hear one lawyer object that the other is "leading" a witness. That objection can be appropriate during direct examination, when the lawyer is only allowed to ask open-ended questions. For a lawyer, it can sometimes be tempting to lead a witness during a direct examination, for example when a witness just does not testify as well as we hoped they would. Sometimes witnesses ramble on, sometimes they lose focus, sometimes witnesses talk about things that we just do not want them to talk about. That is when a lawyer might try to lead that witness during direct examination, and that is when the opposing lawyer jumps up and shouts, "Objection. She's leading the witness."

During a cross-examination, that objection is generally not appropriate because in cross-examination a lawyer normally wants to lead the witness, and is allowed to do so. Cross-examination is used, more or less, as an opportunity for the lawyer to testify and tell your story. The lawyer tells your story by making a variety of statements and forcing the witness to agree or disagree with him or her.

The entire goal of cross-examination is to undermine the testimony that that witness has already given. Sometimes that will be possible; sometimes it will not. It is difficult to undermine the credibility of a priest, for example, whereas the same cannot be said for a former convict. It is difficult to undermine the observations of a police officer who documented his observations immediately after he saw something, while the opposite can be said of someone leaving a bar who had too many beers and was just trying to walk home and happened to see something out of the corner of his eye. The point of cross-examination is to point out those sorts of things—to point out any discrepancies—and demonstrate why the testimony of the witness is not as strong as it might have initially seemed.

Cross-examination can also be used simply to undermine the likeability of a witness. Oftentimes a jury will make a determination about the credibility of a witness based only on whether they like that witness or not.

I recall a time when I stood up to cross-examine a dentist. I certainly had not intended on asking him much, as there simply was not much to cross-examine him about. And I didn't think there was enough important information for me to cross-examine the dentist about without coming across as mean, myself. When I stood up, the first words out of my mouth were, "Good afternoon, Mr. Smith." I certainly meant no disrespect in doing so. And the dentist looked up at me and said only, "Excuse me?" And I said again, "Good afternoon, Mr. Smith." And he looked at me again even more incredulously and said, "Excuse me?" his voice dripping with disdain. I began to worry that I was doing something wrong.

I said, "My apologies, Mr. Smith. I'm just trying to say good afternoon. I'm not trying to fight with you." And that was when he declared with a scowl, "I am a doctor of dental surgery." At that moment I knew that this witness—who had been wholly unimportant two minutes earlier—had just become important. I knew in that moment I could talk to him and make him unlikeable simply through his own personality. What was going to be a two-minute cross-examination turned into a 30-minute cross-examination. And at the end of it, the jury truly disliked him—enough to find in our favor simply so that the dentist would not see any success that day. That was the most fun cross-examination I have ever done. And probably one of the most painful the lawyer on the other side has ever sat through. Word of advice: do not be that witness.

When preparing witnesses for direct examination, your lawyer is going to spend time with those witnesses, talking to them and making sure they not only understand the subject matter they are testifying about, but also understand and recall what they said in the past. I normally try to do that with all of my witnesses, to ensure that they have read their depositions, read the statements that they have made, and are able to testify consistently with those things. I want them to refresh their recollection in time to testify in front of a jury about that subject matter.

We had a trial recently where a witness was testifying about something that occurred years before. This witness had written down statements, given verbal statements, and given a deposition about the incident years before we finally got to trial. Despite our encouraging the witness to make sure he reviewed all the written material that was available to him, the witness decided on his own that he was not going to review any of those materials. He wanted his testimony to reflect what was in his memory at that point in time.

As a result, when he was cross-examined, he gave a lot of "I don't know" and "I don't remember" answers. Those sorts of answers, when there are too many of them, damage a witness's credibility. His credibility was truly harmed by his inability to recall anything when he was cross-examined, because that information was important. His testimony was likely discounted by the jurors, which made for a colossal waste of time, both in preparation and in presenting of his testimony in the first place. On top of all that, it made for a terrible day at trial.

Halftime

Once you and your lawyer have completed a direct examination of all of your witnesses and all of those witnesses have been cross-examined by the other side's lawyer, your lawyer will "rest" your case. Your lawyer will stand up and simply say, "The plaintiff rests." That means that you have presented all of the evidence and witnesses that you believe are needed to support your side of the case. You have presented enough witnesses to tell the story of what happened and describe your injuries and your damages, so that the jury can walk into the deliberation room and answer the questions that the judge is going to provide them.

Once you rest, the judge may entertain motions before proceeding to the defendant's case-in-chief. Usually, those motions are presented by the defendant as a means to short-circuit your case. The defendants will simply argue that there is not enough evidence to prove a particular point or a particular question. The judge will have to rule as to whether the defendant is right, that not enough evidence was presented, or that enough evidence was presented that he can give that question to the jury.

Obviously, that is a very important part of the case. If the defense makes such a motion and the judge grants it, your case can either be ended, or substantially gutted. In those circumstances, you may never have the opportunity to give the case to a jury. So it is very important by that point that your lawyer has covered each and every element of the claim you are making, and presented enough evidence of the damages you've suffered, to give the case to the jury.

Once that process is over, the trial proceeds to the defense's case-in-chief. The process of direct and cross-examination begins again, this time with the defense witnesses. These are witnesses that the defendant wants to present, to prove that you are wrong, that they are right, and that they do not owe you anything. This will follow the same process as before. The defense attorney will conduct direct examinations of their witnesses, and your attorney will cross-examine those witnesses.

Those cross-examinations are the moments when you get to sit and silently cheer while your attorney does to the defense witnesses what the defense attorney did to your own. And if you are lucky, your lawyer is Tom Cruise and he will demand the truth from every single witness that the defense puts up on the stand (although the odds of having the defendant's witnesses arrested after their testimony shall remain very slim).

Once the defense presents all of its witnesses, and all of those witnesses have been cross-examined, the defense will then declare to the judge that the defense rests. But that doesn't mean the trial is over.

Once the defense rests, you as the plaintiff will have one last opportunity to present what are called <u>rebuttal witnesses</u>. Those witnesses can be used to rebut or counter any new issues that the defendant may have brought up during the course of their case-in-chief. In other words, if there was an issue, a fact, or a recollection raised during the defendant's case-in-chief that was not necessarily addressed in your own case-in-chief, you could have the opportunity to present another witness or witnesses to talk about that particular issue.

Once your lawyer is done with your rebuttal witnesses and the defense has had its opportunity to cross-examine those witnesses, the presentation of evidence is over and we move to the next, and almost final, step.

Step Four: Closing Arguments

Once both sides are done presenting all of their evidence and witnesses, the lawyers get to present <u>closing arguments</u>. This is the part of trial that often makes it into the movies and TV shows, and sometimes the nightly news. It is that point where the attorneys get to argue the case to the jury. The attorneys take all the facts of the case, all of the evidence, and apply those facts and the evidence to the law that the judge gives to the jurors. This is the time when real lawyering takes place. For a lawyer, it is probably the most enjoyable part of a case. The lawyer finally gets to tell the jury what the lawyer really thinks about the case.

It is an opportunity to solidify the case in the minds of the jurors, to make sure they remember the story of what happened, and make sure they understand how that story relates to the law. In other words, your lawyer can now use the facts, the witnesses' testimony, and the evidence to make an argument that the defendant was wrong.

Closing arguments are also an opportunity for both lawyers to argue about the amount of damages that could or should be awarded as a result of the jury's determination in the case.

Procedurally, again, as the plaintiff's side, your lawyer will get to go first, and present your closing argument to the jury first. The defendant's lawyer will then follow. Most of the time, a judge will again limit the amount of time that both sides can have in order to present their closing arguments. Those limitations will be based on the complexity of the case, who is involved, how many lawyers might be involved, and things of that nature. Once your side has given a closing argument and the defense has given its closing argument, your lawyer will have the opportunity to present what is called a rebuttal close, using whatever time is remaining. This means that the jury will hear again from your side, which is important. You get to address the arguments that the defense has made, and ensure that the last words the jury hears are from your lawyer, not the defendant's lawyer.

The closing argument is truly the time where your lawyer can take everything that has occurred during the course of the trial and apply it to the decisions that the jury has to make. The sole goal in doing so is to give the jurors the tools they need to answer the questions that the judge has given them—what is the defendant's liability and what are the damages—and answer those questions in your favor.

Your lawyer will employ all the tools and information that you have received during the course of the trial in order to make those arguments. We can even dig back as far as jury selection, and use information we gathered during jury selection in our closing argument.

For example, in a medical malpractice trial we completed, one of the issues was slowing down and taking care when conditions got a little bit rough. I went back to the information we received during jury selection. One of our jurors was a truck driver who was used to driving the mountains of Colorado, in the snow, in the ice, and in the foul conditions that can often hit the roads up there. We used his experience as a truck driver, and made an analogy to the experience of a doctor. I simply said that when you are driving a truck in the mountains and you run into snow and ice, you don't hit the gas and go faster. You slow down, you tap the brakes, you might even stop altogether, until the bad weather passes. We compared that to the conduct of the doctor in the case, who ran into adverse conditions during the course of the surgery, but never took the time to slow down, to hit the brakes, or to stop. The doctor just kept on going.

That analogy hit home. I could instantly see more than one juror nodding their head in agreement with what I was saying. So I knew that I had made a connection. They understood what that case was about simply through the analogy of another juror's experience. It turned out that we were right. We ultimately won that case based on that argument.

The closing argument is the last hurrah for both sides. It is the last opportunity for your attorney to leave it all out on the table, make every argument they can possibly make to support your case, and give the jurors the tools they need to argue on your behalf once they go back to the jury room.

Step Five: Giving the Case to the Jury

Once both sides are done presenting their closing arguments, the case is submitted to the jury, and the jurors take the evidence they need back to the jury room so that they can deliberate. And that is when the waiting begins. The jury is generally not limited in the amount of time that they have to deliberate. They can take ten minutes, or they can take a week. So have a good book ready, because you've probably got some waiting to do.

Joe's Story

The time finally arrived for Joe's day in court, and jury selection began. Judge Claudia Martin called an initial panel of fourteen jurors to find the six people who would eventually decide the case.

Jonathan excused one juror because that juror was a former over-the-road trucker who felt that automobile drivers do not take enough care on the road and cause most of the accidents between truck drivers and cars. He excused another juror who said she believed there are too many lawsuits in the world these days, and seemed more interested in making a political statement by finding against plaintiffs and in favor of defendants. Jonathan excused two others because they had ties to the trucking industry.

The defense attorney, Bob Richardson, struck two jurors because those jurors indicated a preference to simply give Joe money because of his losses, not because they saw any liability in the case. They felt simply because Joe had been injured and his wife killed, that he should receive some money. Bob excused another juror because she was a member of an environmental organization that often campaigned against diesel trucks on the highway. He struck a fourth juror who, like Joe, was an auto mechanic and seemed to empathize with Joe.

The six remaining jurors were sworn in by Judge Martin and the opening statements began. During Joe's case-in-chief, Jonathan presented several witnesses. He called the police officer who had investigated the crash and the eyewitnesses who had been identified in the police report. He called Joe's doctor to testify about Joe's injuries. He called Joe's brother David to testify about the immediate aftermath of the crash and how Joe had been affected by Mary's death. He also called on an economist as an expert witness to testify about Joe's economic losses. Lastly Jonathan called Joe to testify about the effects of his injuries and the loss of his wife.

When it came time to present the case for the defense, Bob put Bill Buck on the stand to give his version of what had happened. He also called an accident reconstructionist to testify about his expert analysis of the incident. Bob also called an economist to rebut some of the evidence given by Joe's economist about the economic losses that Joe had actually suffered.

The trial took about a week—half a day for jury selection and opening statements, then two and a half days for Joe's side of case and another two days for the defense case and closing arguments.

Chapter Eight

The Jury

FINALLY, AFTER THE PRESENTATION of witnesses and evidence and closing arguments, the case goes to the jury. The judge will excuse the jury from the courtroom and send them back to the deliberation room where they will all take a seat, discuss the testimony, consider the evidence, and come to a decision.

Jury Instructions

Before the judge sends the jurors off to the deliberation room, the judge has the privilege of reading to the jurors each of the individual jury instructions that the jurors need to follow during the course of their deliberations.

Jury instructions are generally made up of dozens of different individual laws and rules that the jury has to follow. And so, before the jury can go to deliberate, everyone must sit in the courtroom and listen to the judge recite those rules and laws to the jury, in detail, verbatim, from the stack that he has in front of him.

That can take a long time, depending on how complex the case might be. The judge will read to them rules like, "It is your job to determine the credibility of the witnesses." The judge will also read to them the definition of negligence.

The judge will read to them the instructions that say they have to choose a foreperson. The judge also has to often tell them that their conclusion must be one made by the group and that they must arrive at it together.

All of these instructions are things that have been created after many years of experience. As a result, there is a rule for almost anything that can come up during the course of the trial.

That's why it takes so long to read the instructions. But it is an important step that has to be taken, because odds are good that the jurors are not going to sit back in the deliberation room and read every single rule and law that they have to follow. Hearing the laws and the rules at least once before they go back into that room to discuss the case probably helps things along.

When the jurors go out to deliberate, the jurors can take with them all of the exhibits that have been entered. They take a copy of the law (the jury instructions) that the judge has given them, and lastly they take the verdict form with them. The verdict form will contain all of the questions that the jurors need to answer. That form may be a simple document with one or two questions, or it may be a very complex document with dozens of questions and sub-parts, depending on how complicated the case is and how many claims you have brought against the defendant.

The jury will have as much time as it needs to arrive at a decision. The decision can literally be arrived at in a matter of minutes. It can also be a matter of days or weeks, possibly even months, although it is doubtful that a judge would allow it to go on for that long.

Unfortunately for everybody involved, the plaintiff and the defendant, the only thing to do during that time is wait. There is literally no work to be done either by you, your attorney, or by anybody else while the jury discusses your case and arrives at its decisions. Your patience will be tested.

Jury Deliberations

There are certain steps that the jury goes through in order to arrive at its verdict. One of the first things that a jury will do is choose a foreperson to act as the jury's leader. The foreperson is usually an assertive sort, and they are typically voted on by the members of the jury. Sometimes it is a very simple process. Other times it can be very complicated. But eventually a foreperson is chosen because the judge says that one must be selected.

Once the jury chooses its foreperson, the jury gets to determine its own way of proceeding. There are no rules that dictate to the jury how or when it has to go about making individual decisions for its verdict form. The jury can take votes, they can debate amongst themselves, they can try to convince one another of their positions. Jurors will share their ideas with one another. They will share their doubts, their concerns, and what they think are the strong points of each side's case. It is pure democracy at work. Every member has a voice.

The manner in which they proceed really depends upon the make-up of the jury. You must always keep in mind that these are six or eight or ten individuals who have never worked together before. They likely have never spent time with one another before, and up until that point in time, may not have even spoken with one another, depending on how things have gone during the course of the trial. So jury deliberation is the first opportunity that they have to get to know each other, see who each person is, and learn how each of these individuals feel about the case.

It is important to note that more likely than not, the jurors are not all going to feel the same way about the case. There will be some jurors who are set against you, and there will be some who are for your position. Your only hope at this point is that the jurors who are for you are strong enough in their arguments and in their ability to persuade that they get the jurors against you to come on board with them.

During the time that the jury is out, they cannot talk to the lawyers and they cannot talk to witnesses. The only person they can talk to is the judge, and even then their communication with the judge is very limited. If the jury has a question about something that has happened or they have a question about the law, the jurors can indicate to their liaison—usually the bailiff or court clerk—that they have a question. Typically, those questions have to be written out on a piece of paper and sent to the judge.

When that happens, the judge will ask all the parties to come back to the courtroom and listen to the question that the jury has asked. The judge can only read the question verbatim as it has been written. Usually, the judge will determine what he or she believes the answer to be and then allow the lawyers input, first as to whether or not the question is appropriate and whether it can be answered to begin with, and second, whether the judge's response to the question is the correct one to give. It is usually an informal process, other than having to be conducted in the courtroom. Ultimately, an answer is sent back to the jury, also in written form, so that the jurors can read the answer together and see if it moves their deliberation along.

It is important during this entire process that you stay at the court or someplace very close by, if you can. Do not decide to wait at home. Stay close by. You never know what kind of cues you may pick up on inside the courthouse or courtroom. You never know if a question that is asked will be important, and your presence will help your attorney to read the energy and signals that you may get along the way. Be close by no matter how boring that wait may be. Whether it is a couple of hours or a couple of days, your presence is important.

I have had experience on both ends of that spectrum. I once had a jury come back in 17 minutes with a verdict, which was certainly fast by anybody's standards. I have also had a jury take days.

I was very surprised when I got the verdict in 17 minutes. We assumed when we were being called back in so quickly that we had lost the case. Generally speaking, that is not enough time for anybody to properly discuss all the issues that a judge has given a jury to discuss. But that jury surprised me. It apparently had no doubts at all about anything when the jurors went back to discuss the case. So the jurors were able to answer the questions on their verdict form very quickly. I also suspect they were very much looking forward to going home.

Three days is the longest I have had a jury take to render a decision in a case, and they were three of the longest days that I have experienced as an attorney. It is gut-wrenching, to say the least, as you wait for those individuals to tell you whether the months and years that you put into a case were well spent or not.

In both of these extremes, my clients ended up prevailing and won their cases. Many attorneys will tell you that a short wait in a personal injury case means that the defendant has won, and if the jury is out for anything less than an hour and a half, they are going to come back with a verdict in the defendant's favor. They will also tell you that anything longer than three or four hours is guaranteed to be a plaintiff's verdict—that if the jury is deliberating for longer than that, they are simply talking about how much they want to award in damages.

Some wisdom, based on experience, exists in those rules. But those rules are not hard and fast. And they are certainly not always true. As I said, I have witnessed a verdict come back in 17 minutes and allow for a plaintiff's verdict. I've also seen juries out for two days and come back with a defense verdict (which, thankfully, was not on my case). So there is no firm rule for predicting a verdict based on the time allotted for deliberation. But, if it is a quick verdict, the odds are better that it is going the defendant's way, and the longer the jury is out, the more likely it is that the jury is going the plaintiff's way.

Once the jurors all agree on the answers to each individual question on the verdict form (in some jurisdictions, so long as the majority agrees on the questions on the verdict form), the jurors will complete the verdict form and let the judge know that they are done.

The verdict form that the judge issues to the jury will be unique to each case. As noted previously, it can be as simple as two questions: "Was the defendant negligent? And If yes, then go on to the next question. What are the injuries worth? Economic and non-economic damages." And possibly, "What are the punitive damages?"

Verdict forms can become more complicated depending on how many defendants might be involved in the case, how extensive the damages in the case might be, and whether or not the defendant has raised what are called <u>affirmative defenses</u>—defenses that the jury has to answer about during the course of its deliberations. An affirmative defense does not deny the facts presented by the plaintiff, but offers a set of facts that might reduce or eliminate the defendant's liability.

One other thing that the jury may have to decide during the course of its deliberations, depending on what sort of jurisdiction you live in, is what fault that you may have had in causing your own injuries, whether that is a car accident, or some other sort of incident where you were injured. There is a chance that the jury might be instructed to determine if your own actions played a role in creating your injuries.

In some jurisdictions, if the jury determines that you had any fault at all, you may be barred from any sort of injury award. Those jurisdictions employ "contributory negligence" laws. In other jurisdictions, the jury might determine "comparative fault." In other words, determine what percentage of fault you possess, and what percentage of fault the defendant possesses. Typically, so long as your fault is not over 50 percent, you can still receive an award of damages from the other side, but your damages will be cut proportionately to the percentage of damages for which you are responsible.

In states that have comparative negligence laws, your entitlement to damages will be reduced, based on the percentage of fault that you possess. So, if a jury were to determine you had $10,000 in damages, and you were 25 percent responsible for your own damages, your damages would be reduced by 25 percent, to $7,500, and that is the amount you would walk away with.

Delivering the Verdict

When the jury completes the verdict form and sends it back to the judge, the judge will again call all the parties and their lawyers back into the courtroom, where the verdict will be read in the jury's presence. The jury is then invited back into the courtroom. I can tell you that the jurors' walk from the deliberation room back to the jury box can seem like the longest 30 seconds you have ever experienced.

As the jury walks in, literally all eyes in the courtroom are on them. Every time, I desperately try read some sort of body language or get some eye contact from a juror to get an idea of what the decision is going to be. Everybody—myself and everyone else included—tries to determine what the decision is going to be before it is issued, despite knowing that within a matter of minutes, we'll have the answer. However, I can say that 100 percent of the time, juries are professional in the way they go about their business. I do not remember a time where a juror has decided to make eye contact with me or my clients or with the defendant and the defendant's attorney, or anybody else in the courtroom. Their eyes are all forward. Every juror's face is expressionless, and they walk into the courtroom knowing that they have a surprise for somebody.

I think most jurors understand the gravity of what they are doing. As a result, they act professionally and do not allow their emotions or body language or eye contact to give away the decision before it's time.

Once the jurors are back in the jury box, the verdict form will be handed to the judge, if it has not been already, and the judge then reads the verdict in open court.

From there, the judge will ask the jury if that is, in fact, their verdict in the matter. Most of the time, the answer to that question will be yes. I have yet to have an experience where the answer to that question is no, though I assume it is possible. Once that is done, your trial is complete, for better or for worse.

I should note that there may be an occasion where a jury cannot arrive at a unanimous decision, that there are individuals who might simply not see the case the same way. In such cases, we get a hung jury.

Judges, as you can imagine, do not like hung juries. They like to have a decision one way or another at the end of the day. Before a judge allows for a jury to be officially "hung," the judge will typically give what is called a dynamite instruction, which is an instruction telling each juror that their opinions are very important, but they should sometimes consider the opinions of others in deciding whether they should change their opinion along the way.

It's a thinly veiled attempt to get some jurors, or a juror, to change their position so that the jurors can have a unanimous decision in the case. Sometimes it works. Sometimes it does not. And if it does not, you have a hung jury. Your only option in that event is to start again, and have another trial on another date at another time—a sobering proposition to say the least.

If there is a hung jury, the case will typically stay with the same judge. You will get a new jury, obviously, chosen from a whole new panel, but the case will stay in the same courtroom. And you will try it in front of the same judge again, which may be good or bad, depending on how things went during the first trial.

Oftentimes after a trial, after the verdict is read and the jury's job is done, jurors will want to talk to the lawyers. They will want to talk to the parties about the case and why the jurors came to the decision that they did. It is then that the jurors finally let down their guard. They can be happy moments or sad, depending on the nature of the case. It is always interesting to see those sorts of reactions when the jurors are willing to share them after the course of the trial. Jurors are never required to share their thoughts. When jurors find themselves emotionally invested in the case, they will often stick around and talk to the people involved and explain themselves. I will always take the opportunity if I can get it, because it is helpful. You just don't get it all the time.

Sometimes they do not want to have anything to do with anything that goes on once the trial is completed. In one of my most recent trials, the jurors made a beeline out of that courtroom without talking to anyone. I think to some degree that it had to do with the fact that it was a doctor that they found against. I believe for some people that is an uncomfortable position to be in. Each juror took off right away with the exception of one juror, who hung around and talked to us and told us why the jurors came to the decision they came to.

Most of the time we lawyers do not hear much about the manner in which a case was decided. If a juror sticks around, they talk for a couple of minutes and then go about their way. But a couple of years ago I handled a case for a girl with devastating injuries. It was a two-week-long trial, but we ended up settling the case before the jury came back.

Two weeks later, I ran into one of the jurors at a wedding that we both happened to be invited to. Apparently, we both knew people who knew the same people. It was a unique opportunity to spend 45 minutes talking to this juror about the case, about what she liked, about what she did not like, and how things went. Remarkably, she asked about a particular issue on the case that no one, including myself or any other attorney involved in the case—even the defendant's attorney—had ever picked up on.

It was a piece of video. A girl in the video was carrying a beer bottle, and none of us had noticed it in the two years that we were working on the case. Embarrassingly, not one attorney had ever seen the beer bottle in her hand, despite having watched this video for countless hours during trial preparation. The juror asked, "What about the girl and her beer bottle?" I said, "Oh, no. You're thinking of the guy as he was coming down the escalator." But she insisted, "No. We all saw it." The next day, when I woke up, I went to my computer and loaded that video up again. Sure enough, I could clearly see the bottle in her hand. None of us had ever seen it before.

It is always remarkable, I think, when the jury picks up on an issue or fact we had never thought about or noticed. It happens in every single trial that the jurors find something they think is important or they pick up along the way while they are playing detective. For some reason, because we get so focused on the issues we think are important—the things that we think everybody else should think about—we sometimes miss the little things. And sometimes those little things can be very big deals for jurors and people who had never heard anything about the case until they were called for jury duty.

Rolling the Dice

I should note that a settlement can be reached anytime from the very first day that you contact the defendant and tell them you're thinking about filing a lawsuit, all the way up until the moments before a verdict is read in open court. Truly, anything can happen during that period of time, whether that period of time is six months or 10 years. At any point in time, the parties can come back together and say, "Let's resolve this between us and not roll the dice on a jury verdict."

And it is a roll of the dice. Anytime you give a case to a jury, you are rolling the dice. No matter how well you may have done the job, or your attorney has done the job, there's a chance that a jury is not going to find in your favor. Obviously, there is also a chance that they are. That can make a lot of different things happen, including settlements, just minutes before a jury's about to render a decision in the case.

A Word about the Jury System

Our system—the jury system—is one of the most important and historical systems that our country and our various states have put in place. The jury system literally puts power in the hands of ordinary citizens to determine whether or not what someone did to someone else was acceptable. It takes all the politics out of the decision, and puts the power and the authority to make life-altering determinations back into the hands of the community.

Our founding fathers thought the jury system was so important that they embedded the system into our own Constitution and most states have done the same. It is the one opportunity that ordinary citizens sometimes have to tell a multinational corporation that what it did was not okay, or to tell the government that what it did was not acceptable. A jury will be the most powerful group that most ordinary citizens will ever belong to during the course of their lives. It is what makes our jury system unique and powerful. Many countries don't have juries simply for that reason—because governments do not want to put that kind of power in the hands of ordinary citizens.

But the United States and its individual states have deemed the right to a jury trial to be of paramount importance. It is a right that you get to exercise in the event that you are harmed or damaged as a result of someone else's negligence. But it is a right that not enough of us deem important enough to talk about or defend in the face of the corporate onslaught that is forever trying to undermine that right. It is my hope that you will never have the need to ask a jury to make something right. But if you ever find yourself talking with others about the jury system, defend it as best you can. You never know when you or a loved one is going to need one. And if you do ever need one, you'll be happy that juries exist.

Joe's Story

After Judge Martin gave the case to the jury, the jury began its deliberations. The jury had the case for half of a day when it came time to adjourn for the weekend. On Monday morning, the jurors came back to wrap up their deliberations and finally deliver their verdict.

At long last, Joe finally heard the verdict in his case: The jury found for him and awarded all of the damages he had asked: $2,995,000. There were no legal errors for either Bill Buck or Triple A Trucking to point to during the course of the trial, so neither had grounds for appeal.

Chapter Nine

Resolving the Case

THE DELIVERY of a verdict is not always the end of your case. The case still requires a final resolution. There are several ways for that to happen.

Means of Resolution

Hopefully, your case is resolved is with the jury verdict. In the event that the jury comes back in your favor, and issues a verdict for a specific amount of money to compensate you for your injuries, that can end the case. When that happens, the court will enter judgment on the verdict, and then it is simply a matter of the defendant—or the defendant's insurance company—issuing a check for the amount of the verdict, plus prejudgment interest, and your costs. Ideally, the amount of the verdict will work to make you whole—to allow you to be compensated for your injuries, your pain and suffering, your medical bills, and the economic consequences that you suffered as a result of someone else's negligence.

Sometimes however, a jury verdict is not the final say in the matter. Even if the case goes your way, the defendant can appeal the verdict to a higher court. An appeal is usually a question of some legal issue that the other side believes the judge did not decide correctly during the course of trial. An appeal can follow a verdict for either side, the plaintiff's side or the defendant's side. When either side appeals a verdict, the issue goes to the next highest court above.

Going to an appeals court is not a matter of rehashing the evidence or allowing a jury to find for you again. It is simply a matter of a judge or judges looking at the case, looking at the particular legal issue that a party has raised, and determining two things: First, did the judge in the trial court make an error in allowing things to go the way they did? And secondly, in the event that the judge was wrong in deciding the legal issue that way, did it have an effect on the ultimate outcome of the case?

In answering these questions, the appeals court can uphold the verdict. It can reverse a verdict and send the case back down for another trial. Or it can reduce the amount of damages, depending on the legal argument made. But it is important to note that an appeals court generally cannot increase the damages.

Resolving the Case Through Settlement

Your case may also be resolved by settlement. As noted before, a settlement of the case can happen at any time. It can happen in the moments after filing a demand letter. It can happen on the courthouse steps before a trial begins. It can happen at any point, even after the judgment has been entered by the court. The parties can decide that it's not worth the risks to wait to find out what an appellate court may do with the case, and instead find a place to meet in the middle. That is what a settlement is. It is a compromise—one that you are hopefully approaching from a position of strength.

Normally in a settlement, nobody walks away completely happy. Everyone gets to walk away halfway happy because a settlement is exactly that. It is a compromise. You are giving up something in order to gain some certainty. In the long run, that may or may not be a good decision. But it certainty is a valuable thing when it comes to making a determination of whether you can pay your medical bills or whether you can gain some financial security for the rest of your life, despite your injuries. Certainty can be a good thing. And if both parties can arrive at some certainty, it can sometimes be the best thing.

In the event that you arrive at a settlement in your case, you will be asked to sign a release of claims against the other side. The release of claims is a document which details exactly what rights you are giving up. You will be giving up your right to bring any further claims. You will be giving up your right to a jury trial (if you haven't yet gotten that far).

If there is a settlement, most of the time, there will sometimes be some sort of a nondisclosure agreement that comes along with the settlement agreement. What that means is that going forward, while every side agrees that the case is resolved, you are not allowed to tell anyone other than your spouse, your lawyer, or your accountant how much the case settled for. All you will be able to tell anybody is that the case is resolved.

Once you sign the release of claims, and the nondisclosure agreement if there is one, you will receive the amount agreed upon in your settlement. You can then walk away, and move on with the rest of your life.

Distribution of Funds

If you are fortunate enough to be on the winning side of either a settlement or a verdict, you will ultimately have to deal with the distribution of funds from that judgment. The same distribution process will generally apply, whether it is a settlement or a verdict. Your attorney will handle that distribution.

Generally, the first division of the settlement or judgment will be between you and your attorney. Attorney fees usually come off the top, as a percentage of the verdict or settlement, and the amount that comes off the top will depend upon the agreement that you made with your attorney before ever beginning your case.

Along with the attorney fees, the cost of prosecuting your case will also have to be paid back out of the settlement or judgment. These costs are not the same as attorney fees. Costs are the amounts needed for depositions or trial presentation and other items that your attorney had to pay out-of-pocket in order to prosecute your case. It is always important to remember that these costs will be in addition to your attorney fees.

After the attorney fees and costs are deducted, you may also have medical liens or other liens that need to be paid. Medical liens arise when, because of the injuries that you suffered as a result of someone's negligence, you incurred medical bills. Your insurance may have picked up the cost of those medical bills to begin with, but your insurance company now wants its money back. In most states, they have a right to collect on those funds from the amount that you ultimately get from the defendant or the defendant's insurance company.

You may also have a medical provider who has provided you care on a lien basis. In other words, that provider, knowing that you had a case pending against the person responsible for your injuries, provided you medical care, free of charge at the time, with the expectation that they would be paid back from a final verdict or settlement. Those medical care providers also need to be paid from the proceeds that you receive from your case. In essence, the medical provider has worked on a contingency in the same way that your attorney does.

Generally speaking, if you are getting medical care on a lien basis, the medical care is probably going to cost more than it would if you were paying through insurance. That is because the doctor is taking a risk along with you, knowing that if you don't win your case or settle your case, the doctor will have provided you those services to you free of charge.

Once all of those items are taken out, the remainder of the settlement or verdict amount will go to you to be used as you see fit. Hopefully, your attorney will have some advice for you. If you received a large amount of money, your attorney may be able to provide you with the names and contact information of financial planners or other professionals with the expertise to advise you on ways to invest that money and make it last as long as it can to take care of you and your injuries.

You should also talk to a tax professional. There can be tax implications if the money that is awarded is not for a physical injury. If the money you receive is awarded because of an actual, physical injury that you suffered, that money will probably not be taxable under the IRS code. However, if the damage is awarded for some other reason, if it is for lost wages or some other sort of economic harm that was done to you, those amounts might be taxable. Punitive damages are also taxable. It is very important that you talk to a tax professional before filing taxes for that particular year to determine what portion of that verdict is taxable and what is not.

The End of the Day

As an attorney, meeting with my clients to deliver a check is the most satisfying moment of the whole process—when I can see a client finally get the money needed for the care that they require. It is good to see clients receive compensation to pay for the things that they need, whether that is medical care, a modification to their house to allow them to live comfortably, or just something to make up for the pain and suffering that an accident victim has gone through. Just to see some relief on their faces at the end of the day makes this job worthwhile.

There are many misperceptions out there about successful personal injury cases. Many people see jury verdicts and settlements as some gigantic windfall that accident victims get to blow on vacations and nice cars and an easy-going lifestyle. In truth, that is rarely ever the case. Most of the time, that money is needed to provide for more medical care than what an insurance provider is willing to provide. It can go towards buying a house that somebody needs just to make them comfortable. And it can be used simply to balance the scales of justice for someone who is going to live with physical pain for the remainder of their life.

For example, I recently worked on the case of a girl who was horrifically injured as the result of a car accident. She needed 24-hour care, and that care was being provided to her by her parents. They lived in a small house, which was too small even to modify in order to comfortably house a handicapped patient with a hospital bed and a crane that was needed to lift her in and out of bed or in and out of the shower. The money that the family ultimately received made it possible for them to buy a house that was more suitable to their needs—one that could house a hospital bed, and one in which a track could be installed so that she could be moved to different parts of the house during the course of the day. They received a large amount of money, but it was not a windfall for them; it was simply a means of being able to provide for their daughter the things that she would need for the rest of her life. It was not money for vacations, or new cars, or anything most people would consider a luxury. It was simply money that was being used to make everybody comfortable again. Quite frankly, it simply allowed them to live as close to a normal life as could be expected under their circumstances.

Sometimes, for lower-income clients who are reliant on government-provided healthcare—care that that can be tragically inadequate—a verdict in their favor, allowing them some sort of money, lets them purchase healthcare or insurance in the private marketplace. It allows them to get the medical care they need going forward, paying not just for the medical care they have already received, but for medical care they are going to need down the road. That can lead to a dramatic improvement in the quality of their life, and what they can expect out of their days on this earth.

Joe's Story

Following the trial, Jonathan's office received the check from the defendants' insurance company and distributed the funds from the verdict. The attorney fees and case costs added up to 40 percent of the award. Then the medical liens were paid, totaling $175,000. The remainder of the damages, $1,622,000, went to Joe.

By the time the trial was complete and Joe received his damage award, it was two and a half years after his and Mary's tragic accident. Although Joe would live the remainder of his life without his wife, Joe was confident that he could pay for the remainder of his medical care, and not have to worry about unforeseen medical care down the road.

Conclusion

THANK YOU for taking the time to read this book. It has been a pleasure for me to share my work with you. I love what I do—for me there is nothing more gratifying than seeing a client finally receive justice and compensation after a devastating loss or injury.

I sincerely wish that a book like this would be entirely unnecessary. That people who injure others would simply accept responsibility for the things they have done, or that their insurance companies would accept responsibility for paying for the injuries their insureds have caused. But that thought, I know, is wishful thinking.

We all dread the possibility of serious injury. And I hope that you will never suffer the kind of injury or loss that would require the services of someone like me. But life throws us curve balls and we can never know what to expect. Things happen, even we exercise the most care in our actions. And sometimes those things are serious, even catastrophic events. If that should happen to you, I hope that this book gives you a sense of being at least a bit better prepared if you or a loved one become involved in a potential personal injury case. Know that you do not have to go it alone.

If you've been injured and you feel like you might have a case, please feel free to contact me any time. Even if you just have a question about what you have read here, I am happy to answer the phone. And if I am unable to help you, I will always be happy to help you find someone who can. I look forward to talking with you.

About the Author

Sean T. Olson is a trial lawyer and founding member of the Olson Law Firm. His practice focuses on helping those injured by someone else find justice in state and federal court, by telling effective stories.

Sean tailors his representation to the unique needs of each client, taking the time to determine his client's individual wishes prior to beginning work on a case, to ensure that each client's story is told and heard.

Sean received his J.D. from the University of Denver Sturm College of Law where he graduated near the top of his class. Since 2010, Sean has served as an adjunct professor teaching trial advocacy at his Alma Mater.

Sean is a resident of Denver, Colorado, where he lives with his wife, two young children, and their dogs, Maisy and Charley. Prior to becoming an attorney, Sean was an Emmy-award-winning photojournalist, writer and producer. His passion for that job took him around the globe telling other's stories. He now uses those skills to tell his clients' stories in courtrooms across the country.

www.ingramcontent.com/pod-product-compliance
Lightning Source LLC
Chambersburg PA
CBHW030528210326
41597CB00013B/1073